YOR

n College

College

THE COLOR
PURPLE

ALICE WALKER

NOTES BY NEIL McEWAN

 Longman

 York Press

A00401

We are grateful to David Highan Associates on behalf of the author, Alice Walker, for permission to reproduce extracts from *The Color Purple*, published in Great Britain by The Women's Press Limited, 1983

The right of Neil McEwan to be identified as Author of this Work has been asserted by him in accordance with the Copyright, Designs and Patents Act 1988

YORK PRESS
322 Old Brompton Road, London SW5 9JH

PEARSON EDUCATION LIMITED
Edinburgh Gate, Harlow,
Essex CM20 2JE, United Kingdom
Associated companies, branches and representatives throughout the world

First published 1998
This new and fully revised edition first published 2003

10 9 8 7 6 5 4 3 2 1

ISBN 0–582–78434–4

Designed by Michelle Cannatella
Typeset by Land & Unwin (Data Sciences), Bugbrooke, Northamptonshire
Produced by Pearson Education North Asia Limited, Hong Kong

CONTENTS

PART ONE
INTRODUCTION

How to study a novel 5
Reading *The Color Purple* 6
    Reputation..6
    Womanism..6
    Literary qualities 8
    History..8
    'The Spirit' 9
    Bearings..10

PART TWO
THE TEXT

Note on the text 11
Synopsis 11
The letters 17
Extended commentaries
    Text 1 61
    Text 2 63
    Text 3 65

PART THREE
CRITICAL APPROACHES

Characterisation..67
Themes 76
    Slavery...76
    Feminism..77
    Men 78
    Education and literacy 78
    African-American culture...79
    Business...80
    Violence 80
    Religious belief 81
Narrative techniques 81
    Structure..81
    Coincidence..82
    Letter-writing...82

The Ending 83
Dating events 84
Language and style...86
    Southern dialect..86
    Innocent narrators...86
    Celie's style...87
    Offensive language 88
Symbolism...89
    Purple..89
    Folkspants, Unlimited...90
    Quilts...90
    The Mailbox 91
    Song 91
    Razor 92
    'Dear trees' 92

PART FOUR
CRITICAL HISTORY

....93

PART FIVE
BACKGROUND

Alice Walker 96
    Short Biography 96
    Other works by Alice Walker 97
    Commitments 98
Historical background..99
Literary background 103
Spielberg's film...105
Chronology...108

FURTHER READING 112

LITERARY TERMS...114

AUTHOR OF THESE NOTES 116

INTRODUCTION

HOW TO STUDY A NOVEL

Studying a novel on your own requires self-discipline and a carefully thought-out work plan in order to be effective.

- You will need to read the novel more than once. Start by reading it quickly for pleasure, then read it slowly and thoroughly.

- On your second reading make detailed notes on the plot, characters and themes of the novel. Further readings will generate new ideas and help you to memorise the details of the story.

- Some of the characters will develop as the plot unfolds. How do your responses towards them change during the course of the novel?

- Think about how the novel is narrated. From whose point of view are events described?

- A novel may or may not present events chronologically: the time-scheme may be a key to its structure and organisation.

- What part do the settings play in the novel?

- Are words, images or incidents repeated so as to give the work a pattern? Do such patterns help you to understand the novel's themes?

- Identify what styles of language are used in the novel.

- What is the effect of the novel's ending? Is the action completed and closed, or left incomplete and open?

- Does the novel present a moral and just world?

- Cite exact sources for all quotations, whether from the text itself or from critical commentaries. Wherever possible find your own examples from the novel to back up your opinions.

- Always express your ideas in your own words.

These York Notes offer an introduction to *The Color Purple* and cannot substitute for close reading of the text and the study of secondary sources.

> **CONTEXT**
>
> *The Color Purple* is the third of Walker's five novels.

READING *THE COLOR PURPLE*

How you read *The Color Purple* is up to you. A feminist, an African-American, a civil rights activist, a folklorist, a religious believer and a poet might read with attention to different aspects of the novel. Alice Walker, who is all these things, also stresses the pleasure and power of storytelling, whatever the commitments that inspired a story. As we shall see, a wide range of interest is to be found in what has proved a very powerful story indeed.

REPUTATION

However it appeared to its first readers in 1982, it is hard to approach the novel today without having its reputation in mind. *The Color Purple* almost immediately became a bestseller, a modern classic and a centre of fierce controversy. Winning the American Book Award and the Pulitzer Prize (never before awarded to a **black** woman), it remained on the *New York Times* Bestseller List for over a year. Steven Spielberg's film of 1985 enlarged both the readership and the heated debate that already surrounded the book in the United States.

> **CONTEXT**
> The Pulitzer is the top American literary prize.

Some readers who share Alice Walker's outlook have welcomed the commercial success as an opportunity to spread their views. Others have feared that the desire to write a bestseller may have compromised the author's principles. Some critics, for example, have felt that the **realism** of the early part of the story is sacrificed in favour of the happy ending (see **Critical history**).

The scale of the book's success does seem to have been helped by its double appeal. It can be read as a shocking and subversive assault on 'masculine values', but at the same time it is a romantic and sentimental story of two poor sisters who triumph over adversity. Commitment to a cause and popular storytelling can act as a powerful combination, and Walker's opponents were quick to try to counter the novel's influence.

WOMANISM

Alice Walker's strongest commitment is, in her own term, 'womanist'. At the heart of her story a man is denouncing his wife:

'You black, you pore, you ugly, you a woman. Goddam, he say, you nothing at all' (p. 176). The whole novel can be read as an attack on the assumptions behind these words of Albert to the heroine Celie. Its central theme, that blackness and womanhood are rich and beautiful endowments, is womanist, and aggressively so.

A womanist manifesto is set out as a foreword to Walker's book of essays, *In Search of Our Mothers' Gardens: Womanist Prose* (1983). The term is defined under four heads: (i) 'a black feminist'; (ii) 'a woman who loves other women, sexually and/or nonsexually' (and sometimes also loves men 'sexually and/or nonsexually'), who prefers women's culture, and is 'committed to survival and wholeness of entire people, male and female'; (iii) 'Loves music. Loves dance. Loves the moon. *Loves* the Spirit. Loves love and food and roundness. Loves struggle. *Loves* the Folk. Loves herself. *Regardless*'; (iv) 'Womanist is to feminist as purple to lavender'.

> **CONTEXT**
>
> The novel is set in the golden age of blues and jazz music. Its heroines are womanist in their love of song and dance.

The Color Purple can be read as a celebration of this creed. Celie lives though many misfortunes at the hands of men, including rapes and beatings, and survives to grow into mature and independent womanhood, helped by her love of and sexual relationship with another woman, the singer Shug Avery. In Celie's eyes, and the reader's, Shug becomes a heroic figure, a queen who deserves to be clad in royal purple. For sympathetic readers it can seem, in the words of one feminist critic, 'the perfect emancipation novel' (see **Critical history**). Celie is freed from poverty and degradation, from marriage and from all forms of **patriarchy**.

Not all critics have been sympathetic. In the United States especially, there were strong objections to the lesbian theme and to the remorseless depiction of acts of male violence against women in a novel about black people. Some American critics argued that Alice Walker threatened to divide the black community and detract from the struggle against racism. Her attacks on all forms of male aggression, physical and cultural, found eager defenders, and she has published many accounts of her views on the novel and responses to criticism.

LITERARY QUALITIES

Some admirers and detractors are so concerned with social issues that they treat the novel as a battleground for debate rather than a work of literature with strengths and weaknesses of composition. This is to neglect the fact that *The Color Purple* raises interesting literary questions, too. Various traditions in American literature are combined. One is the **slave narrative**, dating from the eighteenth century. Although the period of history covered in the novel is two generations later than the age of slavery, Celie and her sister Nettie are virtually enslaved in the early part of the story, and they live in a society still suffering from slavery's aftermath.

CHECK THE NET
For Sojourner Truth, see **http://eserver .org/race/aint-i-a-woman.txt.**

Another is the literature of **black** protest, from the days of slavery onwards. Albert's words quoted above, 'You black, you pore, you ugly, you a woman' and Celie's reply, 'I'm pore, I'm black ... But I'm here' (p. 176), are reminiscent of the ironic **rhetoric** of Sojourner Truth (1797–1883), the formidable abolitionist and women's rights activist (see **Further reading**). Alice Walker is also one of the best known of the group of modern African-American women novelists of the South who have emerged during the last twenty-five years and who share an admiration for the work of Zora Neale Hurston (?1901–60). These and other elements in Walker's reading are discussed later (see **Literary background**).

HISTORY

The Color Purple can be read as a historical novel. The story begins in the early years of the twentieth century and, following the life of Celie, covers several decades of life in the American South, emphasising the hardships and joys of black people, and especially of black women at the hands of men. The story of Nettie, a missionary in Africa, surveys the colonial period with an equally feminist stress on the oppression not only of Africans by Europeans but also of African women by African men. Early-twentieth-century history at home and abroad, the novel asserts, shows the sorry mess that men have made of the world.

History in Alice Walker, and especially in this novel, aims to be unconventional, and inclined to mock at masculine conceptions of

Great Men. *In Search of Our Mothers' Gardens* (1983) records how the 'germ' of the story was a remark about a pair of female drawers. Walker remembers how 'a black male critic ... said he'd heard I might write a historical novel someday, and went on to say, in effect: Heaven protect us from it.' She laughed over this because 'womanlike (he would say), my "history" starts not with the taking of lands, or the birth, battles and deaths of Great Men, but with one woman asking another for her underwear' (pp. 355–6).

CHECK THE FILM
Contrast the different tone of images and music in the opening scene of Stephen Spielberg's film, *The Color Purple.*

It could be argued that one of the novel's strengths is its amalgam of historical survey with an everyday perspective, focused on underwear and kitchen floors, and the feelings of the people closest to such real things. The way that Celie's character is developed through the evolving language and style of her letters is also impressive. As Celie becomes more literate, she grows in confidence, raising her head in the world (see **Text 2, Extended commentaries**).

'THE SPIRIT'

Celie begins by writing to God. A new preface to the 1992 (tenth anniversary) edition of *The Color Purple* complains that critics have neglected the theme of religious faith. Celie and Nettie are deeply pious women, and Alice Walker conveys their feelings from memories of her own Christian upbringing. She has rejected Christianity (calling herself 'a born-again pagan') in favour of belief in 'the Spirit' (to whom the novel is dedicated), and maintains that religion should be taken out of churches and returned to nature. Shug Avery teaches a similar, **pantheist** faith in the novel, and Celie comes to accept it.

Some feminists may agree with Shug that traditional Christian language and **imagery** are misleading where they imply that God is an old white man. Others may feel that Walker is a better poet than theologian, and that the evocative symbol of the colour purple enriches the novel more effectively than vague talk about the Spirit. With Alice Walker, there is always plenty of opportunity to disagree (see **Themes**, on **Religious belief**).

CHECK THE NET

To find out more about Alice Walker, see **www. sistahspace.com/ sistory/writers/ walker**.

BEARINGS

For feminists, even for those who distance themselves from Alice Walker's position, this novel has already become a classic. Readers other than feminists are likely to be drawn into the story by the life and wit of her writing. Celie's people are all excellent talkers, and she has an amazing way with words. This is a very polemical book, but it has many other qualities, polemic aside, as we shall see, including a distinctive warmth and tenderness, and a disarming sense of fun.

THE TEXT

NOTE ON THE TEXT

The Color Purple was published in the United States by Harcourt Brace Jovanovich, New York, 1982. It was published in Great Britain by The Women's Press, London, 1983, and has been constantly reprinted ever since. A new preface was added in 1992 to mark the tenth anniversary. These Notes are based on the text of the British edition.

The letters are not numbered in any edition of the novel. For study purposes it is very convenient to number the letters, although in writing about the novel it should never be implied that they figure in the text. Students numbering the letters 1–90 for use with these summaries must remember that each letter begins on a fresh page. Page numbers are given for the beginning of each new letter. Letters quoted within letters are not to be numbered.

SYNOPSIS

The story begins in the first decade of the twentieth century. The setting is rural Georgia, and the characters are black Americans. Celie (who is never given a surname) is fourteen years old. Her mother is mentally disturbed. We find out later that this is due to the death of her father, lynched twelve years ago by white business rivals. Celie thinks that her mother's second husband, Alphonso, is her father. She has a younger, much loved sister, Nettie, and numerous small half-brothers and sisters. When Alphonso rapes her she writes a letter to God, asking for a 'sign', because she cannot understand what has happened. This begins a sequence of fifty-one letters from Celie to God, written at intervals over a period of more than thirty years.

Celie's mother dies. Alphonso takes away the two children, a girl and a boy, that Celie bears him. He threatens to rape Nettie, but

> **CONTEXT**
>
> Celie writes in dialect. Her early letters are movingly simple in style. Later her powers of expression develop remarkably, although she never quite conforms to standard English.

Celie intervenes, offering herself in her sister's place. When Celie is about nineteen, Alphonso marries her to a local farmer. Celie calls her husband Mr — (afraid to use his first name, Albert). Her husband treats her brutally, often beating her, and she works in his house and on his farm almost as a slave. One day she sees her daughter, now aged six, and the woman who, with her clergyman-husband, has adopted the child, who is called Olivia. Nettie comes to live with Celie but is soon obliged to flee from the advances of Mr —. Celie advises Nettie to seek out the couple who have adopted Olivia.

Mr — has four children by his former wife and Celie cares for them. The eldest boy, Harpo, grows up and marries Sofia, a strong, independent-minded woman who loves, but refuses to live in subjection to, her husband. She retaliates very effectively when Harpo tries to beat her. Celie is at first envious of Sofia's free spirit, but they are reconciled after a quarrel and become friends.

CONTEXT

Shug is a successful blues singers, and so belongs to a far wider social world than the one Celie knows.

Celie and Mr — have one thing in common: both are infatuated with the famous singer Shug Avery. Mr — has been Shug's lover, and they have had children together. Celie has only seen her in a photograph. When Shug falls ill, Mr — takes her in and Celie nurses her. Celie is sexually attracted by Shug and devoted to her, and through her devotion they become friends. When Shug says 'Albert', Celie realises that she had forgotten his first name. Sofia has wearied of Harpo's bullying, and goes to live with one of her sisters with their five children. Harpo converts the house into a jukejoint: a bar with music and dancing. Shug sings there, dedicating a song to 'Miss Celie'.

Sofia returns one evening to the jukejoint. She quarrels with Harpo's girlfriend, Mary Agnes, nicknamed Squeak, and knocks her down. A few days later she quarrels with the wife of the white mayor and, when he strikes her, Sofia knocks him down. She is arrested, badly beaten and sentenced to twelve years' imprisonment. After three years she is placed in the mayor's household as a prisoner-maid to his wife Miss Millie. Shug leaves Celie and Albert, and tours the country as a singer, growing famous and rich.

Years go by. One Christmas, Shug returns with a husband, a toothy, vulgar man called Grady. When Grady and Albert stay out all night drinking, Shug and Celie share a bed, for warmth. Celie tells of how Alphonso abused her. Shug comforts her and they make love.

Shug discovers that Nettie has been writing to her sister for more than twenty years and that Albert has been hiding the letters. She and Celie find bundles of letters in a trunk. A sequence of these letters to Celie now tells us what has become of Nettie. The preacher, Samuel, and his wife Corrine, the couple who adopted Olivia and Celie's other child Adam, have taken Nettie into their household, and she has gone with them as a missionary to Africa. She describes conditions among the Olinka tribe where they have lived and worked ever since. The Olinka are a poor but independent people until the building of a road and the introduction of rubber plantations, to benefit faraway foreign interests, destroys their way of life.

> **CONTEXT**
>
> The 'Olinka' are a typical West African people. No particular region is intended.

Corrine notices how closely the children resemble Nettie and is jealous, supposing Nettie to have been Samuel's lover. She accepts the truth only on her deathbed. Nettie now learns that Samuel was formerly acquainted with Alphonso, and knows the facts about the sisters' parentage. Nettie and Samuel go to England to try and help the Olinka, and there they marry. Unfortunately, their efforts on behalf of the Olinka are unsuccessful, and they return disappointed. Adam falls in love with an African girl called Tashi, and becomes distressed because she has her face scarred in a traditional ceremony. Missionary work becomes unfeasible in this part of Africa, and the family hope to return to America.

Nettie's letters are interspersed with letters Celie writes to her. Celie is overjoyed to find that Alphonso is not their father. Shug talks to Celie about religion, and persuades her that God is not to be pictured as a wise old (white) man, but worshipped as a power in Nature and a spiritual force within us. Sofia is released from service in the mayor's house. Mary Agnes becomes a professional singer. She goes off to Panama with Grady, and Sofia returns to Harpo. Celie announces that she means to leave Albert and go to live with Shug in Memphis. She curses her husband and he denounces her as a

CONTEXT

Memphis, Tennessee, on the Mississippi River, was the birthplace of the blues and a centre of the music recording industry.

poor, ugly, black woman, that is to say 'nothing at all' (p. 176). Celie proves him wrong when she goes to Memphis, where she runs a successful business called 'Folkspants, Unlimited', and lives happily with Shug. It is Albert who goes into a decline, having to be nursed back to health by Harpo. He only recovers when he returns the remainder of Nettie's letters to Celie, and is thus freed from his wife's curse.

Alphonso dies. Celie and Nettie inherit land and a business, formerly their father's and willed to them, but withheld by Alphonso. Celie is heartbroken when Shug falls for Germaine, a young man in her band, and tours the country with her new boyfriend. Sofia's sixth child (not Harpo's), Henrietta, becomes sick, and Celie nurses her. There is a false report of Nettie's death in the Atlantic (by this time the Second World War has started). Shug leaves Germaine and returns to Celie. Albert is now a reformed character; he has even taken up sewing. He and Celie have friendly talks; she even mentions his name, but there is no chance of a revival of their marriage. Celie tells him frankly that she has always found men physically unappealing.

The last letter sees the reconciliation of all the principal characters. Nettie and Samuel, Adam and his wife Tashi, with Olivia, come safely home, and Celie has a family at last. This, the ninetieth letter, is addressed to 'Dear God. Dear stars, dear trees, dear sky, dear peoples. Dear Everything' (p. 242), and offers thanks for happiness at last.

TIME SCHEME

Dates are very approximate (see Dating Events)

Letter 1 **1904–5**	Celie is aged fourteen	**Letter 31** **1922–3**	Sofia leaves Harpo
Letter 2 **1905–6**	Death of Mama	**Letters 37–41** **1924**	Sofia is sent to prison
Letter 9 **1910**	Celie marries Albert	**Letter 43** **1927**	Sofia becomes a nursemaid
Letter 10 **1911**	Celie sees Olivia, aged six	**Letter 45** **1934**	Shug, married to Grady, comes for Christmas
Letter 11 **1912**	Nettie runs away	**Letter 49** **1935**	Celie receives her first letter from Nettie
Letters 54–5 **1913–14**	Nettie arrives in Africa	**Letter 74** **1936**	Sofia is released from prison
Letter 18 **1917**	Harpo marries Sofia		
Letter 22 **1921**	Shug comes to stay with Albert and Celie	**Letter 80** **1939**	Nettie marries Samuel
		Letters 88–90 **1941–2**	Resolution

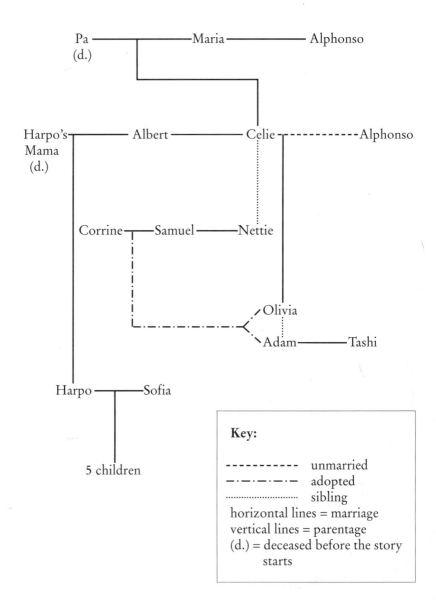

Pa (d.) —————— Maria —————— Alphonso

Harpo's Mama (d.) ——— Albert ——— Celie -------- Alphonso

Corrine —— Samuel ——— Nettie

Olivia

Adam ——— Tashi

Harpo ——— Sofia

5 children

Key:

- - - - - - - - - - unmarried
— · — · — · — adopted
· · · · · · · · · · · · · · sibling
horizontal lines = marriage
vertical lines = parentage
(d.) = deceased before the story starts

THE LETTERS

LETTER 1 (PAGE 3)

GLOSSARY
Lucious Lucius
kine kind

- 'Dear God, What is happening to me?'
- Celie has been raped by her stepfather.

A fourteen-year-old girl is writing to God because she has no one else to confide in. She does not give her name; we learn in Letter 7 that she is called Celie. The reader understands from what she says that Celie has been raped by a man called Alphonso ('Fonso'), apparently living with her mother, who has been resisting Alphonso's advances and was away visiting a doctor at the time of the rape. We learn in Letter 6 that Celie believes the man to be her father. (He eventually turns out to be her stepfather.) She is shocked and distressed. She hopes that God will send her 'a sign'. Her mother, she says, is too ill to live long.

COMMENTARY

The **point of view** is that of a naive first-person narrator. The girl describes what happened to her in blunt but innocent terms. It is obvious that she does not have a concept of rape or understand the probable consequences.

CONTEXT

Mention of the town of Macon sets the scene in Georgia, Walker's home state.

We notice non-standard features of language indicating southern American dialect speech, especially in the use of verbs, but many sentences are normally formed, including, for example, the first three (see **Critical approaches**, on **Language and style**). The point of view remains that of Celie confiding in God until Letter 52. Other voices are heard as Celie remembers them, her mother's, and Fonso's, here, those of Mr — and other characters later.

LETTER 2 (PAGE 4)

- A year later, Celie is pregnant for a second time and fears that Alphonso will kill this baby too.

This must be a year later, because Celie is pregnant for the second time. The birth of the first baby astonished Celie. When her mother asked who was responsible, she said that God was. Alphonso took the baby away and, she believes (wrongly, as we find out in Letter 10), killed it in the woods. Celie told her mother that 'God took it'. Her mother has since died, in agony and rage, and it seems that Alphonso felt some genuine grief at her death. Celie tells God that she fears Alphonso will kill her next baby too. Meanwhile she has to keep house, and act as nanny to all her smaller brothers and sisters.

COMMENTARY

Contrasting this summary with the text of the second letter shows the extent to which the reader is obliged to interpret the narrator's anxious, urgent messages to God. She assumes that God will understand everything. We need to work out the sequence of events.

LETTER 3 (PAGE 5)

- Alphonso is now eyeing Celie's younger sister Nettie.

CONTEXT

Monticello, and Gray (mentioned in the next letter) are towns in Georgia.

More months have passed. Alphonso has not killed Celie's second baby, but sold it to a childless couple living some distance away. Alphonso tells her she is 'evil', 'disobedient' and 'indecent' because she has milk running down her body and no proper clothes. He does nothing to help her. She hopes he will marry again soon. He is looking lustfully at Nettie, Celie's younger sister. Nettie is afraid, but Celie means to protect her, God willing.

LETTER 4 (PAGE 6)

- Alphonso has married again.
- A widower is interested in Nettie.

GLOSSARY

in the same shape of the same age and build
more than a notion a serious undertaking

Celie is reluctant to give Alphonso a name, usually writing only 'he', but in this letter she calls him 'Pa'. Pa has brought home a new wife, a teenage girl of about Celie's age. This girl seems to like her husband, but is bewildered by her new duties in a house with so many young children. A widower with three children is interested in Nettie, and he visits her every Sunday. Celie calls him Mr —. His wife was killed 'by her boyfriend coming home from church'. Celie is sure that Nettie will do better to continue attending classes at the local school, rather than submit to such a marriage.

COMMENTARY

It is not until Letter 82 that Celie learns that Alphonso is not her father.

LETTER 5 (PAGE 7)

- Celie is not attracted by men, only by women.
- She hopes to save Nettie from Alphonso.

GLOSSARY

story lies

Alphonso has beaten Celie, she reports to God, for winking at a boy in church. She did not wink, and she does not look at men. She looks at women instead. She finds women more attractive because they do not frighten her. She mentions that God might be surprised at this, because her mother used to curse at her so much. She denies that she feels angry with her mother, blaming her Pa's lies for her mother's death. When she sees Pa eyeing Nettie, she stands in his way. She advises Nettie to marry her admirer, because that will save her from Pa. She says that Nettie may be able to enjoy one more year of her youth before the pregnancies begin. Celie does not expect to become pregnant again.

LETTER 6 (PAGE 8)

GLOSSARY

somethin tail animal fur

- Alphonso does not allow Mr — to marry Nettie.
- Celie is attracted by a photograph of the singer Shug Avery.

Mr — asks Alphonso for Nettie's 'hand in marriage'. Alphonso refuses on the grounds that Nettie is too young and Mr — has too many children. His last wife, furthermore, died in scandalous circumstances. There are further scandalous rumours about a liaison between Mr — and a woman called Shug Avery.

CONTEXT

Cars were a recent invention at this date, a sign of Shug's wealth and glamour.

Shug Avery interests Celie and her 'new mammy', who manages to obtain a picture. Shug turns out to be a beautiful woman, rouged and dressed in furs, with a certain sadness about the eyes. The photograph shows her in front of a motor-car. Celie is fascinated by this romantic image. She stares at the photograph every night, and dreams about Shug – 'dressed to kill', and dancing and laughing.

GLOSSARY

horsehair worn as a hair-piece

trampy behaving like a prostitute

God done fixed her it is believed that she is now infertile

it bees it is. Shug's eyes seem to say that insults from men are an inevitable part of life

crib barn

LETTER 7 (PAGE 9)

- Alphonso offers Celie to Mr — in place of Nettie.

We learn Celie's name, and that she is now nearly twenty. While her new mother is sick, Celie has to protect Nettie from Pa by offering herself instead. To make herself more alluring, she dresses herself up as well as she can. She succeeds in rescuing her sister, although she also suffers another beating and sexual assault for her effrontery.

Mr — calls again, terrifying Nettie. Alphonso, however, refuses to part with Nettie, saying that he means to make a schoolteacher of her when she has had some more education. In her place he offers Celie. He tells Mr — that although she is ugly and not a virgin, Celie has two advantages: she works hard, and she is not able to bear any more children. Obliged to listen to this account of herself, Celie finds consolation in gazing into the sad but powerful eyes of Shug Avery in the treasured picture. Alphonso offers to give Celie a dowry: her own linen and a cow. Mr — is left to consider this handsome offer.

COMMENTARY

We learn Celie's name by chance when she mentions how Alphonso spoke of her. Celie's avoidance of it up to now suggests her low self-esteem. Her unwillingness to name men, saying only 'he' or 'Mr —', suggests her negative feelings about them. She names Nettie and Shug repeatedly and possessively.

Alphonso's contempt for women appears in his references to 'a fresh one'. He speaks of Celie and of his wife as though of animals or slaves.

> **CONTEXT**
>
> Linen and a cow are details that contrast backward, rural Georgia with Shug's social background, evoked by the photograph.

LETTER 8 (PAGE 11)

- Mr — agrees to marry Celie.
- Celie and Nettie are studying hard.

Spring has gone by, and Mr — has decided to marry Celie. She thinks only of Nettie, whom she hopes to be able to save from Alphonso. Perhaps this will be easier, she tells herself, when she is married to Mr — since he obviously still prefers Nettie. The sisters may be able to run away together. Meanwhile they are working hard at Nettie's schoolbooks, trying to make themselves well enough educated to survive in the world on their own if they do run away. Celie has not been to school since the time of her first pregnancy (five years ago), since her love of school means nothing to Mr —. He ignored Nettie's pleas on her sister's behalf, and those of the teacher, Miss Beasley, dismissing her as a garrulous spinster. Miss Beasley gave up her attempts to intervene when she saw that Celie was pregnant.

Mr — comes to make a final inspection of Celie. She has to turn about before him while he sits on his horse and Alphonso reads his

> **GLOSSARY**
>
> **Columbus ... Santomareater** Christopher Columbus (1451–1506) sailed from Spain in 1492 with three ships: the Santa Maria, the Pinta, and the Niña
>
> **Indians ... queen** Columbus took slaves back from the New World as one of his gifts for King Ferdinand V and Queen Isabella of Spain, who had financed his voyage
>
> **run off at the mouth** talks too much
>
> **bout the ground ... flat** that the earth is a sphere
>
> **drug out** exhausted
>
> **nary one of them** not one of the children

newspaper. Mr — agrees to take Celie as his wife only when he is reassured that the cow is still included in the bargain.

COMMENTARY

Celie's ironic remark on how flat the world looks to her is a sign of her improving powers of self-expression. The description of Celie standing before Mr — while he looks her up and down is one of many which imply that Celie and Nettie are treated like slaves (see **Themes**, on **Slavery**).

LETTER 9 (PAGE 13)

- Married to Mr — and lying in bed with him, Celie thinks about Shug Avery.

Celie is married. On her wedding night Mr —'s eldest boy, a twelve-year-old, throws a stone which cuts her head. His mother died in his arms, and he wants no stepmother. It turns out that Mr — has four children, all hard work to look after. Celie lies in bed with Mr —, thinking about how to keep Nettie safe. Then she thinks about Shug Avery, who perhaps used to enjoy what Mr — is now doing to her. This thought makes her put an arm around her husband.

COMMENTARY

We discovered how the child's mother was killed by her boyfriend in Letter 4. The brutal behaviour of Mr — is reinforced by the image of Celie's bandaged head on this loveless wedding night.

LETTER 10 (PAGE 14)

- Celie finds her daughter Olivia.

Celie sees a little girl bearing a strong resemblance to herself and to Alphonso, walking in town behind the woman who has adopted her (or bought her). She is about the right age to be the baby taken from Celie six years ago. Celie's heart tells her that this is her first child.

Olivia's new mother is buying cloth in the store. Celie approaches and finds out that the new father is a clergyman. The storekeeper speaks contemptuously to both women (in a manner that suggests he must be white) and they leave. Since the Reverend Mr — has not yet arrived, they sit in Celie's husband's wagon to wait. As they talk we learn for the first time that Celie's husband is a handsome man. She admits that men all look alike to her. Her daughter's adoptive parents have named the little girl Pauline, but given her the pet name of Olivia. The Reverend Mr — makes a brief appearance, a large man. Olivia's new mother has a lively sense of fun. When Mr — returns, he finds to his annoyance that Celie is bursting with laughter.

COMMENTARY

'Girl' (p. 14) is a contemptuous form of address to a black woman. See Letter 71 for a comment on the offence this incident causes (see **Themes**, on **Slavery**).

GLOSSARY (cont)

clam climbs

don't hit on much don't look smart

git it understand the word-play on 'hospitality'

CHECK THE FILM

In Spielberg's film, the insolent storekeeper is seen to be white.

LETTER 11 (PAGE 17)

- Nettie runs away from Alphonso and comes to stay with Celie and Mr —.

Nettie comes to stay with Celie and her husband, having run away from Alphonso. Her presence is a comfort to Celie, to whom she passes on what she has learned at school. Nettie urges Celie to control the children with a firmer hand, and to try to fight in the battle of life; Celie says she only knows how to survive. She still cares more about Nettie than about herself, and is afraid that her sister's talents will be lost if she has to marry a man like Mr —.

Mr — has agreed to let Nettie stay because he hopes to seduce her. When she resists his advances, he says she must leave. There is an

GLOSSARY

they mean they are inconsiderate

to make miration over to make a fuss about showing admiration emotional parting. Celie advises her to seek the help of the Reverend Mr — 's wife – the only woman Celie has ever seen allowed to handle money for herself. Celie says she will not be alone so long as she can spell G-o-d. They agree to write to each other. But after Nettie has gone, no letters arrive.

COMMENTARY

We learn why no letters arrive from Nettie in Letter 50: Mr — intercepts and hides them. This is one of the **melodramatic** features of the plot.

LETTER 12 (PAGE 19)

- Two sisters come to stay.

Carrie and Kate, two of Mr — 's sisters, come to stay. They praise Celie's housekeeping warmly, stressing this as a duty of all married women, sadly neglected by Mr — 's previous wife, Annie Julia. She had not wanted to marry Mr — at all; once married, he continued his pursuit of his former lover, Shug Avery, with no regard for his wife's feelings. Celie is a wife to be valued: tireless in keeping house, cooking and tending the children.

Kate comes again, this time alone, and urges her brother to buy his wife some clothes, instead of keeping her in rags. When Kate takes her to buy the clothes, Celie daydreams about Shug Avery. She considers what colour of dress Shug Avery would wear. Shug is like a queen to Celie, and so she thinks it would be purple, the royal colour, with maybe a little red to brighten it. But Mr — is unlikely to waste his money on such expensive colours, so Celie settles for blue, and is overcome with the dress – the first that has ever been made for her.

Kate tells the eldest boy, Harpo, to help Celie with the chores. Harpo refuses, saying that such work is only fit for women. When Kate insists, Harpo tells Mr —, who sends her home. Kate offers Celie the advice she has already received from Nettie: she should learn to fight for herself. Celie says nothing, but thinks that by doing as she is told, she will at least stay alive. Nettie tried to fight, and now (so Celie thinks) she is dead.

COMMENTARY

The contrast between Celie's rags and Shug's finery (like royal robes) is reminiscent of fairy stories (such as Cinderella).

LETTER 13 (PAGE 22)

- Harpo learns about how to treat a wife.

Harpo is curious to hear about how wives are best managed, and asks his father, who tells him they must be beaten, especially when they are as stubborn as Celie. Celie tries to make herself wooden, like a tree. This, she says, is how she knows that 'trees fear man'. Harpo tells Celie that he is in love with a girl. He has only winked at her in church, but he tells Celie that they plan to marry, although he is only seventeen, and she fifteen, and he has not yet spoken to her. This may be why he has asked his father's advice about wives.

COMMENTARY

On a second reading of the novel we notice Celie's remark that 'trees fear man' because it foreshadows the theme of roofleaf and Nettie's account of the destruction of trees in Africa, in Letters 61 and 80.

LETTER 14 (PAGE 22)

- Harpo learns about how to treat a wife.

Shug Avery is coming to town to sing at the Lucky Star saloon. Celie and Mr — are very excited. Mr — dresses carefully, for once.

GLOSSARY
bug round
yall you (plural)
Amen corner at prayer

CONTEXT
'Yall' is the dialect form for 'you all', usual in Southern American usage (and preferred by Walker to 'you guys').

GLOSSARY
orkestra a blues band
hick country bumpkin
like Indian Chiefs covered with feathers
Queen Honeybee because she is sweet; 'Shug' is an abbreviation of Sugar

CONTEXT
Blues singing
originated in the
Southern states in
the nineteenth
century and
became widely
popular after
1900.

Pink posters, picturing Shug as 'Queen Honeybee', are fastened to trees. Celie has no hope of attending a performance, but dreams of seeing Shug perform.

COMMENTARY

Shug's stage name of 'Queen Honeybee' recalls the royal or noble titles bestowed on top blues singers and jazz musicians by their fans: Bessie Smith was 'Empress of the Blues' (see Letter 33) and the band leader Edward Ellington was 'Duke' Ellington (see Letter 46).

GLOSSARY
**Where you all
children at ...?**
where are your and
Shug's children ...?

Feel like snakes evil
thoughts

LETTER 15 (PAGE 26)

- Celie works while Mr — mopes.

Mr — spends the weekend in town, returning tired and sad. Celie longs to question him about Shug. She works long hours in the field chopping cotton, unaided by Mr —, who makes a feeble attempt to help before returning to the veranda to smoke his pipe and stare into space.

LETTER 16 (PAGE 27)

- Mr — is still lovesick.
- Celie and Harpo do all the work.

The lovesick Mr — now sits hopelessly all day, staring at nothing. Harpo, afraid of his father, is obliged to do all the ploughing. Wife and son labour like slaves. Celie thinks that Harpo's weakness makes him look womanly. Harpo is still in love.

LETTER 17 (PAGE 28)

- Sofia makes her presence felt.

Harpo's girl's father rejects him as a suitor because his mother's murder is still reckoned a disgrace. Harpo suffers nightmares, reliving the scene of his mother's death. The 'boyfriend' shot her in the stomach and she died in Harpo's arms. Waking in the night, Harpo trembles and protests to Celie that his mother was not to blame.

Celie is kind to Mr —'s children, but has no affection, or any other feeling about them. Harpo continues to confide in her, however, praising the beauty of his girl, whom he now names as Sofia. He hopes that he will be regarded as a more acceptable husband once he has succeeded in making her pregnant. Once she is pregnant, he brings her to visit his father. They come marching up the road, hand in hand, Sofia in front. She is a large, strong girl, intelligent and independent, quite unafraid of Mr —. She has left home, but is living with her married sister; she tells Mr — that she will wait there until Harpo is allowed to marry her.

CONTEXT
'Bright' skin meaning 'lighter coloured' is a reminder of the African American viewpoint in this novel, where white skin is the only strange sort.

COMMENTARY

After Sofia's departure, the men are at a loss what to do or say, for once, because they are unaccustomed to such an outspoken woman.

LETTER 18 (PAGE 32)

- Harpo marries Sofia.

Harpo marries Sofia; the baby in her arms is a big 'nursing' boy. He brings them back to a small house on his father's land, which they repair. Harpo begins to receive wages and he works more willingly. Sofia remains a strong, confident girl, and they are happy together. Only Mr — is cynical about their future.

LETTER 19 (PAGE 34)

- Celie betrays Sofia.

Trouble comes from Harpo's fixed idea that Sofia ought to obey him. She loves him, but has no intention of behaving like the submissive Celie. Mr — disapproves. Wives are like children, he says, and must be beaten if they are to be kept in order. Celie thinks that the marriage, now three years old, would be a happy one if Harpo would only forget his father's teaching and accept Sofia as she is. But Celie also resents Sofia's independent ways, and especially dislikes seeing Sofia pity her. When Harpo asks for advice, she tells him to beat Sofia. The next time she sees Harpo, his face is a mass of bruises. He tells unlikely tales about a mule and a barn door. Sofia retains the upper hand.

COMMENTARY

It is an especially clever detail to make Celie advise Harpo to beat Sofia. It is a lifelike moment of weakness (afterwards bitterly regretted) and true to the behaviour of oppressed people who sometimes do fall into the oppressor's ways of thinking.

LETTER 20 (PAGE 36)

- Sofia proves more than a match for Harpo.

Harpo and Sofia continue to have fist-fights. Celie witnesses one appalling contest, where they tear their house apart, and which Sofia wins. She and Harpo, with the two babies, leave in the wagon the next day, as she wanted, to visit her married sister.

LETTER 21 (PAGE 37)

- Sofia proclaims that women must learn to fight

Celie has trouble getting to sleep for over a month and decides that she is suffering for her sin against Sofia. She hopes that Sofia will not find out that she advised Harpo to use violence. Harpo tells, however, and Sofia is furious. Celie confesses that she is jealous of Sofia's ability to fight for herself. Sofia talks about her childhood. She was one of twelve children, six girls and six boys. The girls were obliged to learn to fight, and to stick together. No girl is safe from her own male kin, Sofia says, unless she can fight. Celie says, piously, that life is short, but Heaven will be for ever. Sofia recommends bashing Mr —'s head open, and thinking about Heaven later. They collapse in laughter, and then set to work on quilt-making. Celie can sleep once more.

LETTER 22 (PAGE 40)

- Shug falls sick.
- Albert brings her home.

Shug is ill, and everyone has turned against her, except Mr — and Celie. The preacher at church and her parents at home have condemned her, but Mr — goes off in his wagon and brings her home five days later, sick and stumbling, but still 'dress to kill' (p. 41). Celie is fascinated by the 'mean' look on Shug's now feverish face, and by the enigmatic tone of her cackling voice. Her greeting is 'mean': 'You sure *is* ugly' (p. 42).

GLOSSARY

witch hazel a herbal remedy for ills

Bible say … mother see Deuteronomy 5:16

Old Maker God

CONTEXT

The traditional art of quilt-making provides a happy opportunity for women to work together and is a symbol of female solidarity.

GLOSSARY

got his mouth on speaks against

amen all through the novel 'amen' tends to imply mindless religious conformism, although not in Letter 75 or at the very end

mean American usage has the senses of 'hostile', 'malicious', 'troublesome' and 'hard to defeat'

LETTER 23 (PAGE 43)

- Albert nurses Shug devotedly.

Shug is sicker than Celie's mother on her deathbed, but she is more 'evil', Celie says, and that keeps her alive. Her strength of will is undiminished. She hectors Mr —, whom she calls Albert, even forbidding him to smoke in her sickroom, where he mopes in the shadows. Celie is astonished to see how easily he can be subdued. She had forgotten his name. She notices for the first time that Albert has a weak chin. It is also the first time that he and she share a concern, in their common devotion to Shug. He consults Celie, for once, asking her if she minds having Shug in the house.

COMMENTARY

Although Celie continues to speak of Mr — until almost the end of the novel, the reader is likely to follow other characters in thinking of him as Albert. He seems less of a monster from now on. He sheds a tear of sympathy for Shug at the end of this letter.

GLOSSARY
bat her eyes flutter her eyelids

CONTEXT
'Ma'am' is a reminder of the social distinctions of the time. Shug is used to the easier manners of show business.

LETTER 24 (PAGE 45)

- Celie bathes Shug and falls in love with her.

Although Shug and Albert have had three children together, he is uncomfortable about giving her a bath, so Celie has to do it. When Shug is naked for her bath, Celie is so attracted by the sight of her long body that she wonders if she has turned into a man. Her hands tremble as she washes her patient. They begin to talk. Shug rejects Celie's deferential 'ma'am'. She tells Celie she never misses her children, who live with their grandmother.

COMMENTARY

Celie's powers of expression have been improving and this letter, where she discovers her own sexual nature, is full of examples of her growing fluency and her imaginative use of figurative language (see **Text 1, Extended commentaries**).

LETTER 25 (PAGE 46)

- Shug recovers.

Shug refuses food, confining herself to coffee and cigarettes while she looks through fashion magazines, seeming to be puzzled by their images of white women in high society. Celie tempts her successfully with the smell of home-cured ham. This puts Celie and Albert in so good a humour that they laugh together. Albert looks slightly crazy because he has been so afraid.

COMMENTARY

The pictures in the magazine are an indication that we are now in the 1920s.

CHECK THE FILM

The song 'Miss Celie's Blues' is one of the best songs in Spielberg's film.

LETTER 26 (PAGE 48)

- Shug composes a song for Celie.

Shug begins to get better, tended by the attentive, loving Celie. She treats Shug with the care she would like to show her daughter Olivia. Shug composes a song inspired, she says, by Celie.

LETTER 27 (PAGE 49)

- Albert's father is a most unwelcome visitor.

Albert's father arrives; a small, pompous and indignant man. While he denounces Shug, Celie spits in his glass of water and wonders how to prepare ground glass. Albert's brother Tobias is the next visitor. He brings a ridiculously small box of chocolates and a large amount of vulgar curiosity. Celie teaches Shug to sew quilts. Sitting between Shug and Albert, united with them in opposition to Tobias and all the outside world, she feels happy.

COMMENTARY

This letter incident brings Albert and Celie closer than ever before, in shared hostility to the old man and loyalty to Shug.

GLOSSARY
You feeling yourself
Sofia thinks Celie is talking nonsense
Clabber curds
troth trough

CONTEXT
The joke that Harpo's fatness makes him look pregnant is one of several playful hints that he and Sofia might exchange sexes.

LETTER 28 (PAGE 53)

• Harpo is overeating.

Sofia and Celie work on a quilt. Sofia is worried about Harpo, who has become absurdly gluttonous, consuming vast amounts of fattening food. Harpo likes housework and Sofia likes working outdoors, so they ought to get on well together, but Harpo is obviously unhappy about something. He gorges between meals, and, the women agree, has started to look pregnant. Celie watches him with concern.

LETTER 29 (PAGE 56)

• Celie urges Harpo to accept Sofia's independent nature.

Harpo breaks down in tears one night when he is staying with Albert and Celie. He tells Celie how much he wants Sofia to obey him, or at least pay some attention to what he tells her. Sofia refuses to 'mind' (p. 57) him, and she blacks his eyes when he tries to beat her. Celie urges him to accept Sofia as she is, a good wife who loves him. Harpo seems unable to take this advice.

LETTER 30 (PAGE 58)

- Sofia intends to leave Harpo.

Celie visits Sofia. It seems that Harpo is overeating because he hopes to match his wife's weight and improve his chances in their up to now unequal combats. But Sofia is weary of Harpo's obsession with power: he wants a dog, not a wife, she says. She intends to take the children and move to her sister's home. Celie is shocked, but also filled with envy at the idea of having such a refuge. Sofia still loves her husband but their sexual relations are now cold and unfulfilling. All that she really wants is a change of scene for a while.

GLOSSARY

shingles thin oblong pieces of roofing material

like running ... on itself her love for another woman seems to lead nowhere

LETTER 31 (PAGE 60)

- Sofia leaves Harpo.

Sofia's sisters arrive in strength to escort her. Celie presents her with the finished quilt. Powerless to stop his wife's departure, Harpo is a sorry sight as he says goodbye to his children, changing the baby for the last time and drying his tears on the nappy.

GLOSSARY

seining netting

Dilsey, Coco and Boo the names of their cows

LETTER 32 (PAGE 62)

- Harpo opens a jukejoint.

Six months have passed since Sofia left. Harpo is greatly changed. Having been thoroughly domesticated as a husband, he is now determined to make money and is converting his house into a jukejoint where his friend Swain will play jazz and people will come out from town for dancing and entertainment. He seems sure Sofia will not return.

GLOSSARY

jukejoint a bar and dance-hall

CONTEXT

Jukejoints had to be out of easy reach of the police because of Prohibition, the law banning the sale of alcohol in the United States, in force 1920–33.

GLOSSARY

box guitar

chitlins chitterlings, fried pork intestines

shifts dresses

Bessie Smith (1894–1937) a brilliant entertainer and singer; known as 'the Empress of the Blues', she was immensely successful in the 1920s.

sassy cheeky

www. CHECK THE NET

For all about Alice Walker's connection with the blues, see **http://www.sistah space.com/sistory/ writers/walker/ youjust.html**.

CHECK THE BOOK

The American dramatist Edward Albee (b.1928) based his play, *The Death of Bessie Smith* (1960), on the popular (although mistaken) belief that her life might have been saved after her fatal motor accident if a hospital for whites had admitted her.

GLOSSARY

lightening bugs fireflies

LETTER 33 (PAGE 63)

• Shug sings 'Miss Celie's song' at the jukejoint.

In the first few weeks nobody comes to Harpo's jukejoint, apart from friendly visits by Albert and Shug. Then Harpo recruits Shug as a singer. Posters go back on the trees. The bar is filled to overcrowding on Saturday nights. Celie is not allowed to go to such a low establishment; she longs in vain to hear Shug sing. Then Albert's objections are overruled by Shug herself, and Celie goes to a performance. She is jealous because Shug seems to have eyes only for Albert. Then Shug sings 'Miss Celie's song', the one Celie helped her to compose.

COMMENTARY

'Miss Celie's song' (p. 65) is a love song, a symbol of the bond that now unites Shug and Celie. Shug's formal 'Miss' is itself a mark of her respect and love. Celie has never been so highly regarded or so happy.

The mention of Bessie Smith, Empress of the Blues, is a further reminder of the cultural background of the 1920s. Bessie Smith's song 'A Good Man is Hard to Find', sung here by Shug, was recorded in 1927, with Porter Grainger on piano and Lincoln Conoway on guitar.

LETTER 34 (PAGE 66)

• Shug and Harpo are in business together.

Shug sings every weekend at Harpo's place and they both make good money. Singing restores Shug to full health and she decides to leave. When she hears Celie's fear that Albert will start beating her again once she has gone, she promises to stay until she can be sure that he will not do it.

LETTER 35 (PAGE 68)

- Shug makes Celie jealous by sleeping with Albert.

Celie is jealous because Shug is now sleeping with Albert. When she discusses this with Shug, she conceals the fact that it is Shug, not Albert, she wants to keep for herself. Shug tries to explain her passion for Albert: he is small and amusing and 'smells right'. She is amazed by Celie's confession that she has never enjoyed sexual relations with men. She tells Celie this means she is still a virgin, and begins to teach her about sexual pleasure. Celie still feels jealous at night.

GLOSSARY
rassle rustle
not with my sponge and all refers to her method of contraception

LETTER 36 (PAGE 71)

- Trouble at the jukejoint.

Sofia returns. She appears at the jukejoint with Henry Broadnax, known as Buster, a man who looks like a prize-fighter. Sofia and Harpo dance, until Harpo's girlfriend, known as Squeak, quarrels with, and slaps, Sofia. Sofia's tough upbringing has made her return any blow by instinct. She knocks Squeak down, dislodging two teeth.

GLOSSARY
white lightening corn whiskey
scandless scandal
teenouncy cheeky

LETTER 37 (PAGE 75)

- Sofia is in prison after striking the mayor.

Celie advises Squeak to make Harpo call her by her real name, Mary Agnes, because that will make him take her seriously when he is in trouble. Trouble has come: Sofia is in prison. Celie relates to Mary Agnes how Sofia met Miss Millie, the mayor's wife, who made a fuss of her children and then asked if Sofia would care to work as

GLOSSARY
going on over colored making a fuss over black people
Just long ... colored so long as Albert remembers the difference in status between the white sheriff and himself
eggplant aubergine, coloured purple

her maid. Appalled at the thought of becoming a white woman's servant, Sophia replied, 'Hell, no' (p. 76). The mayor slapped Sofia, who knocked him down. Celie cannot go on with the story, so Albert tells how the police beat Sofia before they arrested her, their guns on Buster, the prize-fighter. Mary Agnes runs to comfort Harpo. Albert persuades the sheriff to allow a prison visit.

Sofia is badly injured and bruised purple all over. Celie attends to her as well as she can.

COMMENTARY

This letter marks a turning point in the plot, and begins the section of the novel concerned with Sofia's sufferings and endurance as a victim of injustice.

LETTER 38 (PAGE 78)

- Sofia begins a twelve-year sentence.

The prison visits take place twice a month for half an hour. Sofia works in the prison laundry, in horrible conditions. She learns to behave like Celie, always obedient. But the twelve years of her sentence are 'a long time to be good', as she ruefully jokes. Mary Agnes is helping Sofia's sister Odessa to look after the children.

LETTER 39 (PAGE 80)

- Sofia's friends take counsel.

Celie, Shug, Mary Agnes, Odessa and two more of Sofia's sisters, Albert and the prize-fighter meet to discuss what to do, because they fear for Sofia's sanity. Harpo and the prize-fighter dream of violent action. Celie dreams of rescue by angels. A practical plan is devised when it is realised that the light-skinned Mary Agnes is related to the white prison-warden, Bubber Hodges. Bubber is her uncle.

COMMENTARY

This letter makes the ironical point that 'black' and 'white' people, social worlds apart on grounds of 'colour', were often closely related.

LETTER 40 (PAGE 82)

- Mary Agnes visits the prison warden.

Mary Agnes is dressed as a white woman, except that the clothes are patchier. The plan is for her to remind the warden that they are related and that he once gave her a present when she was a child. She must then persuade him that Sofia is quite happy in the laundry, but would loathe being forced to work as a white woman's maid: that would be a real punishment. The idea behind the plan is that the warden will believe that Mary Agnes wishes Sofia harm as she lives with Harpo, and as her kinsman he will fulfil her wish and make Sofia a maid.

LETTER 41 (PAGE 83)

- The warden commits 'a little fornication'.

The warden is not pleased to be reminded of his kinship with Squeak. He listens to her story, and then asks her to undo her clothing and commits what he calls 'a little fornication' (p. 84). She goes home with her dress torn. She has suffered in a good cause, however, and has acquired a new self-confidence, in spite of humiliation. When Harpo says he loves her, she demands her rightful name, not Squeak but Mary Agnes.

COMMENTARY

Mary Agnes's demand to be called by her right name is one of several places in the story where a name or the form of a name is meant to be telling (see **Critical approaches, Characterisation**).

LETTER 42 (PAGE 85)

- Mary Agnes becomes a singer.

Six months pass, and Mary Agnes becomes a singer. Her small, high voice seems odd after Shug's singing, but she soon becomes popular. She is still angry about the teeth that were knocked out, but she helps to care for Sofia's children all the same.

LETTER 43 (PAGE 87)

- Sofia is a nursemaid for Miss Millie's children.

Three years later, the prison authorities have followed Mary Agnes's suggestion and transferred Sofia from the laundry to duties outside the prison as nursemaid to Miss Millie's children. The mayor's six-year-old son shouts orders, and tries to kick Sofia. She moves out of the way, and the boy hurts his foot. Sofia would be blamed if it were not for the little girl, Eleanor Jane, who dotes on her nurse and testifies to what really happened. Sofia has recovered her physical health, but she broods on violent revenge.

LETTER 44 (PAGE 89)

- Sofia sees her own children for fifteen minutes.

The mayor has bought his wife a new car, but he declines to teach her to drive. Sofia, who used to drive Buster's car, gives Miss Millie lessons. In return, Miss Millie drives Sofia home to spend Christmas Day with her family. She is a well-meaning but ineffectual woman, who does not let Sofia sit beside her in the car because that is 'not done in the South'. As things turn out, Millie's incompetence spoils Sofia's one holiday, and she manages to spend only fifteen minutes with her family.

CONTEXT

The convention of things 'not done in the South' was for a long time used as an excuse for racist behaviour.

LETTER 45 (PAGE 93)

- Celie is jealous because Shug has married.

The story of Celie and Shug is resumed; we can work out later that several years must have passed since the last letter. Shug comes to stay for Christmas and brings a surprise – a new husband. He is a toothy, vulgar man called Grady whom Celie instantly dislikes. She and Albert are extremely jealous. Rich and famous, Shug is driving a new car. She is slow to greet Celie, but does so warmly.

LETTER 46 (PAGE 95)

- An unhappy Christmas.

The men drink their way through Christmas, while the women work, talk and celebrate. Shug seems indifferent to the pain she is causing Albert and Celie. Celie confesses that she still is, in Shug's sense, a virgin.

GLOSSARY

Sophie Tucker (1884–1966) black American singer, actress and entertainer.

Duke Ellington Edward Kennedy 'Duke' Ellington (1899–1974), black American band leader.

CONTEXT

Duke Ellington was the most influential composer and arranger in the history of jazz. His compositions include 'Mood Indigo'.

LETTER 47 (PAGE 96)

- Shug sleeps with Celie, who relates her early sufferings.

Albert and Grady go off in the car and Shug sleeps with Celie for warmth. Celie tells her how she was raped by Alphonso when she was fourteen, and she recalls the horror of those days as she lies in Shug's arms. They make love.

GLOSSARY

like somebody from the North attempting to appear sophisticated

LETTER 48 (PAGE 98)

- Shug encourages Mary Agnes to start a singing career.

Sleeping with Shug feels like heaven to Celie. It lasts until the men return at dawn, when Albert falls into bed, drunk and snoring. Grady annoys Shug by calling her Mama, and by making eyes at Mary Agnes. Shug is generous to her, however, and encourages her to start a career as a professional singer.

GLOSSARY

mailbox on a post by the road, well away from the house

a little fat white woman the Queen of England, we learn in the next letter, although the King's head would have appeared on British stamps at any date during the period covered by the novel

LETTER 49 (PAGE 100)

- A letter from Nettie.

Celie has a letter from Nettie at long last. Celie has told Shug about the mystery of Nettie's failure to write. Shug has seen Albert pocketing letters with foreign stamps. We can guess why Nettie's letters have never reached Celie. Nettie's letter shows that she has guessed too: Albert must have been intercepting her letters. She continues to write at Christmas and Easter, just in case one might get through. She says that Celie's son and Olivia are alive and well and coming home soon.

COMMENTARY

Another major turning point in the story is reached here. From now on, groups of Nettie's letters alternate with Celie's, and so, therefore, does the narrative **point of view**. The African part of the story henceforth counterpoints the American (see **Themes**, on **Slavery**, and **Text 2** of **Extended commentaries**).

CONTEXT

Queen Victoria (short and plump) reigned 1837–1901.

LETTER 50 (PAGE 102)

• Shug relates her early life.

Shug has become friendly with Albert again. She walks to the mailbox with him. This is how she secured Nettie's letter. Celie is so angry about Albert's theft that she is in danger of cutting his throat until Shug takes the razor from her. Shug tells Celie about her early life. Her puritanical mother soon rejected her. She found comfort in loving Albert, who joked and danced better than anyone when he was young. Shug bore him three children. When she was finally turned out of the house by her parents, she went to live with a 'wild' (p. 104) aunt in Memphis, Tennessee. Albert married Annie Julia because his father insisted that Shug was 'trash' (p. 104) and Albert was too weak to stand up for himself. Shug regrets her heartless behaviour to Annie Julia. She is puzzled by Albert's cruelty to Celie.

GLOSSARY

reefer of cannabis

Lillie the first mention of her Christian name

the moochie the partners in this slow dance stand very close

CHECK THE BOOK

For more about the moochie, see Alice Walker's essay 'Anything We Love Can Be Saved' in her book of the same title (1997).

LETTER 51 (PAGE 106)

• A cache of Nettie's letters is found.

Celie and Shug find bundles of letters from Nettie in Albert's trunk. They steam the envelopes open and reclaim the contents, replacing the empty envelopes in the trunk.

LETTER 52 (PAGE 107)

- Nettie's letter from years ago urges Celie to leave Albert.
- Nettie is staying with the clergyman who adopted Celie's child.

In this letter from Nettie to Celie, Nettie urges Celie to leave Albert. She relates how Albert followed and tried to rape her on the day she fled from his house. She fought him off. In fury he threatened that neither sister would ever hear from the other again. Nettie has reached the Reverend Mr — 's house, and found Olivia there.

COMMENTARY

Nettie's letters take us back in time. This letter must have been written soon after Nettie ran away. As the novel progresses, Nettie's letters become gradually more recent, until the sisters are united in time as well as place at the close (see **Critical approaches, Narrative techniques,** on **Dating events**).

LETTER 53 (PAGE 108)

- Nettie helps Samuel and Corrine in their church work, and lives as a member of the family.
- Olivia has a brother, Adam.

From Nettie to Celie, a few weeks later – Nettie begs for a letter as soon as possible. The woman Celie met in the store is called Corrine and her husband is called Samuel. The little girl is now known as Olivia. There is also a little boy called Adam. The family are kind to Nettie, involving her in their work for the church.

COMMENTARY

We learn that Adam is Celie's son in the letter after next. The significance of his name appears in Letter 87.

LETTER 54 (PAGE 109)

- Samuel and Corrine are to go to Africa as missionaries.

From Nettie to Celie – Nettie is very worried about Celie's failure to reply and about her own situation. She is unable to find suitable work. Corrine and Samuel are about to go to Africa as missionaries. She begs for a letter.

LETTER 55 (PAGE 110)

- Nettie is in Africa. She means to write regular letters to Celie even though there is no reply.

From Nettie to Celie – Celie's headnote to this letter tells us that it is dated two months after Letter 54. Nettie is now in Africa. She wrote almost every day of the journey, but destroyed these letters in a moment of despair. Now she has decided to write to Celie in the same desperate hope that made Celie start writing to God. She describes a meeting she had before leaving with a woman who we know from her description must be Sofia (at the time she worked as Miss Millie's nursemaid). She then hears from Samuel and Corrine about how this lady came to be imprisoned. This episode inspired her to accept Samuel's invitation to accompany the family to 'the middle of Africa' (p. 112) as a missionary. She assures Celie that Olivia and Adam are her children and that they are growing up happily.

COMMENTARY

Unusually, a reference is made to the date of this letter: 'dated two months later'. That implies that the earlier letters were dated within a shorter space of time. At the time this letter was written, less than a year can have passed since Celie and Nettie parted (see **Critical approaches, Narrative techniques**, on **Dating events**).

> **GLOSSARY**
> **Atlanta** the state capital of Georgia
> **Milledgeville** a town in Georgia

> **CONTEXT**
> 'The middle of Africa' is meant to remain a vague location. A British colony south of Liberia would have extended inland from the West African coast.

GLOSSARY

gored formed with wedge-shaped panels of cloth

boater a flat straw-hat

Harlem the section of New York City between East River and Harlem River at the northern end of Manhattan Island

Speke John Hanning Speke (1827–64), British explorer. He found and named Lake Victoria [Victoria Nyanza], and explored the upper waters of the Nile

Livingstone the Reverend Dr David Livingstone (1813–73), British missionary and explorer

Stanley Sir Henry Morton Stanley (1841–1904), British explorer and journalist. He was foreign correspondent for the New York Herald when he met Livingstone, then exploring the sources of the Nile, and greeted him 'Doctor Livingstone, I presume?' at Ujiji, on Lake Tanganyika, in 1871

vesper service evening church service

LETTER 56 (PAGE 113)

● Nettie visits Harlem and admires the dignity of its residents.

From Nettie to Celie – Nettie feels one of the family rather than a maid; she studies and she teaches the children. She describes her stay in New York before boarding the ship, and praises Harlem, where black people live with dignity and faith. The enthusiastic support and generous fund-raising of church people in Harlem is contrasted with the cold and haughty manners of white people in the Missionary Society.

LETTER 57 (PAGE 116)

● Nettie describes the voyage to Africa.

From Nettie to Celie – Nettie praises Samuel's wisdom and kindness. She is enthusiastic about the ship on which they crossed the Atlantic, and about the strange ways of England, where some fund-raising was done. She is beginning to learn about the colonial history of Africa. She has discovered that slaves transported to America were often bought from within the slave trade practised by Africans. The journey from England is via Lisbon, Dakar and Monrovia.

LETTER 58 (PAGE 119)

● Nettie visits Senegal and Liberia.

From Nettie to Celie – she recounts more about the journey, including the stop in Senegal, then a French colony, and the visit to Monrovia. Nettie finds that there are many white men in Africa, and that not all are missionaries. The president of the Africangoverned state of Liberia seems remote from the problems of his people. Nettie hears the singing of exhausted workers in the cacao fields and learns that the plantations are Dutch-owned. She ends by describing the intense emotion of homecoming when she, Corrine and Samuel first saw the coast of Africa and gave thanks to God.

COMMENTARY

Some white people in West Africa at this date were Christian missionaries; others were colonial officers, concerned with administration and justice; others again represented foreign companies such as the Dutch owners of the plantations mentioned in this letter, which begins the criticism of bad government and commercial exploitation continued in Nettie's later letters (for more on colonial West Africa, see **Historical background**).

LETTER 59 (PAGE 122)

- Shug comforts Celie.

Celie resumes her letters to God. When Shug pleads with her not to murder Albert, on the grounds that his removal would leave her only Grady to sleep with, Celie begs Shug to sleep with her in future, and Shug agrees.

LETTER 60 (PAGE 124)

- Celie starts her pants-making career.

Celie and Shug sleep together 'like sisters' because Celie is too angry, at the thought of the letterless years, to make love. Shug persuades her to sew herself some pants; her dress is unsuitable for work in the fields, and pants will suit her.

GLOSSARY

J. A. Rogers Joel Augustus Rogers (1883–1966), historian and journalist. His 'From Superman to Man' was published in 1917. His controversial views on African history met with opposition

Senegalese Wolof and Fulani are spoken in Senegal

Tubman this must be a predecessor of the noted President (William V. S.) Tubman (1895–1971), who took office in 1944

cacoa the cacao tree; its seeds are used to make cocoa and chocolate

Thou Shalt Not Kill see Matthew 19:18

pants slacks or casual trousers (US)

CONTEXT

Harlem saw a renaissance of music, arts and literature in this period.

CONTEXT

Liberia was a state created for former slaves who wished to return to Africa.

Letter 61 (page 126)

GLOSSARY

dunces she fears they may be mentally handicapped

pidgin English a trade-language

bush forest or uncultivated countryside

palm wine made from fermented palm sap

cassava … yam plants with starchy tubers

millet a type of food grain

CONTEXT

The Olinka people venerate the leaf as a symbol of divine protection.

CONTEXT

Pidgin draws grammar and vocabulary from English and other languages; it often serves as a medium between speakers of different West African languages.

• Celie frets about her children's parentage.

Celie is looking forward to Nettie's return, but is beginning to worry about her children, fearing that their conception (which she believes to have been incestuous), may have injured their development. She quotes within this letter to God an entire letter from Nettie.

Nettie describes how they left the ship at a small port somewhere in West Africa and were led to the village where they are to work. The land of Olinka is described. The people are amazed by the sight of the women missionaries, and they gather round Nettie and Corrine, touching their dresses and hair. Their guide, Joseph, explains that the missionaries who have come before were all white, and furthermore, only men have come until now. The Olinka ask questions, and one comments that the two children resemble Nettie, not Corrine. The Olinka are healthy but very poor by American standards. They harvest enough yams, cassava and other produce to keep them self-sufficient. They count themselves rich in roofleaf, which is both the covering for their huts and their 'god'.

COMMENTARY

Mention of roofleaf's significance in Olinka religion prepares for the catastrophe in Letter 80, pp. 192–3, when tin is provided for the roofs of workers' huts. Nettie's sympathy with African religion develops in the course of her letters (except when it is an obstacle to women's emancipation), as she witnesses colonial disregard for traditional beliefs and as her own faith becomes less doctrinaire (see **Text 2** of **Extended commentaries**).

LETTER 62 (PAGE 132)

- Nettie faces difficulties in her work.
- Corrine is beginning to be jealous.

From Nettie to Celie – Nettie seldom has time to put pen to paper, but whatever she is doing, she is writing to Celie in her mind. She writes realistically about West African insect bites and other difficulties of settling in, including cultural differences. Olivia is the only girl in the village school because the Olinka believe that education should be for boys alone. Olivia compares this narrow-mindedness with that of 'white people at home who don't want colored people to learn' (p. 133). She hopes that she and her Olinka friend Tashi will grow up to have more interesting lives than women are allowed in the village. Corrine is becoming jealous of Nettie as a rival. Domestic troubles seem to be in store.

COMMENTARY

Comments on education help to link thematically the African and American parts of the story (see **Themes**, on **Education and literacy**).

GLOSSARY

Schweitzer Dr Albert Schweitzer (1875–1965), German theologian, philosopher and musician, who abandoned a brilliant career in 1913, to run a mission-hospital at Lambaréné (in present-day Gabon)

LETTER 63 (PAGE 136)

- Olivia's friend Tashi learns Western ways.

From Nettie to Celie – Tashi's parents complain that Olivia's influence is distancing their daughter from the life and customs of the Olinka people. Nettie tells Tashi's father that Africa is changing and will soon be more than just a man's world. He defends the dignity of Olinka women; superior, he says, to the condition of an outcast and drudge such as Nettie. He says he is willing to receive Olivia in his house, where she will be able to learn true womanly ways.

GLOSSARY

GLOSSARY

Uncle Remus Joel Chandler Harris (1848–1908) published 'Uncle Remus, his Songs and Sayings' in 1881, and the classic series of Uncle Remus books followed. An old black American tells stories to a small boy. Like Alice Walker, Harris was born in Eatonton, Georgia (but see **Background**, on **Commitments**)

Keening lamentation for the dead

CHECK THE BOOK

Among the animal characters drawn from African folklore in the *Uncle Remus* books are Brer [Brother] Rabbit and Brer Fox.

LETTER 64 (PAGE 139)

• Nettie thinks about her life in Africa.

From Nettie to Celie – five years more have passed. A road is being built through the forest. The Olinka welcome the road-builders with gifts and friendship. Corrine is growing more jealous of Nettie, and has asked her not to invite Samuel to her hut. Nettie now values the company of her niece and nephew more than ever. Tashi has lost her father, who died of malaria. Nettie broods about the lives of Olinka women, who seem happy although they have to share husbands and cannot have men as friends. She thinks the women spoil their husbands and that this makes the men 'childish' (p. 141). She also notes that Olinka men have the power of life and death over their women.

LETTER 65 (PAGE 143)

• Colonial rule brings many difficulties.

From Nettie to Celie – another year has passed. The road the Olinka welcomed has flattened most of their village. The whole region, furthermore, has been bought by a British company and the forests are being cleared for rubber plantations. The chief's appeal to the governor only resulted in a demand for taxes. Essential village buildings, including the school, have been rebuilt, however; several girls now attend the school. Corrine has been ill.

LETTER 66 (PAGE 146)

• Corrine's jealousy increases.
• Rubber plantations ruin the Olinka hunting grounds.

From Nettie to Celie – times are becoming ever more difficult.

Corrine frets because the children resemble Nettie. She demands that Nettie and Samuel swear on the Bible that they never had an affair. The fields and hunting grounds of the Olinka have been destroyed to make space for planting rubber.

LETTER 67 (PAGE 148)

- Nettie has learnt from Samuel that she and Celie are not Alphonso's children.

From Nettie to Celie – Samuel has always thought that the children must be Nettie's. That is why he first took her in and later invited her to go to Africa. Samuel turns out to possess crucial information about the sisters' background. When he was a young man, he used to be acquainted with Alphonso. He is sure that Nettie and Celie are the children not of Alphonso but of a trader lynched by white rivals. Alphonso married this man's widow, who was afflicted by mental illness. This woman must be Celie and Nettie's mother and Alphonso their stepfather. Nettie prays that this letter may reach Celie with the wonderful news that 'Pa is not our pa!' (p. 150).

> **CONTEXT**
>
> Lynching, or hanging without trial, was common practice in the old South.

LETTER 68 (PAGE 151)

- Celie is amazed and delighted.

This brief note is Celie's last letter to God until Letter 90. It records her amazed and delighted discovery that her children were not incestuously conceived, and that all her assumptions about family have been turned upside down. Shug is going to take her away, to Tennessee. She ends by telling God that he must be asleep, to have kept all this from her.

GLOSSARY

bought me my own white boy hired a white man as an assistant

cockleburrs prickly plants

CONTEXT

Alphonso characteristically uses the language of slavery ('bought'…'boy').

LETTER 69 (PAGE 152)

• Alphonso confirms that he is not the sisters' father.

From Celie to Nettie – Celie visits Alphonso. She and Shug drive there in the Packard, wearing their new 'flower pants' as emblems of liberation. There are real flowers everywhere about them as they drive through the countryside on the new tarmac roads. Alphonso seems to be enjoying great prosperity; he has a new, fifteen-year-old, wife. He has a white man working in his store. He says that he kept the true story of Celie's parentage secret because it was too sad to tell to little girls. Shug and Celie look for but cannot find the graves of Celie's parents.

LETTER 70 (PAGE 157)

• Corrine is dying.

From Nettie to Celie – Corrine is dying. Nettie has told her about the children's parentage, but she cannot believe it, or remember the meeting with Celie in the store (in Letter 10).

GLOSSARY

hitching post to tie horses

appliquéd in needlework, pieces of one material applied to the surface of another

Spelman Seminary see **Background**, on **About the Author**

LETTER 71 (PAGE 159)

• Corrine dies, acknowledging that Nettie has told the truth about the past.

From Nettie to Celie – Nettie has tried to make Corrine remember. She has found in Corrine's trunk the quilt she made from the cloth she bought the day she met Celie; this revives a memory long suppressed, as Corrine now admits, because Celie was so like Olivia. She recalls the incident with the white storekeeper that Celie writes of in Letter 10. Corrine dies just after acknowledging that Nettie has told the truth.

COMMENTARY

Corrine's deathbed reconciliation and her convenient removal from the story to allow for Nettie's marriage to Samuel are reminiscent of conventions of **closure** in Victorian fiction, and in popular entertainment today.

LETTER 72 (PAGE 161)

- Corrine is buried.

From Nettie to Celie – Corrine is given a traditional Olinka funeral. Samuel and the children feel their loss keenly. Nettie dreams of seeing Celie again. Two ill-mannered white men have been to survey the village. Nettie has told Samuel about her letter-writing.

COMMENTARY

Female genital mutilation, a topic alluded to in this letter, is a major theme in Alice Walker's novel *Possessing the Secret of Joy* (1992), where Adam and Tashi appear as characters (see **Background**, on **Other works by Alice Walker**).

LETTER 73 (PAGE 164)

- Celie and Shug talk about God.

From Celie to Nettie – Celie has stopped writing to God because, she says, 'if he ever listened to poor colored women the world would be a different place' (p. 164). In spite of her reputation as 'a devil', Shug dissuades Celie from blasphemy. They discuss religion. Celie admits that her idea of God was a mental picture of an old

GLOSSARY

my friend menstrual period

one ritual circumcision

CONTEXT

Faces are painted white at the funeral; it is the colour of death and mourning in many parts of Africa.

grey-bearded white man. Shug tells her that God is not a person outside her but a power within. God can be seen in the beauty of nature. He can even be known through sexual pleasure, 'some of the best stuff God did' (p. 167). Shug believes that God wants to be admired. She says, 'it pisses God off' (p. 167) if people pass a field of purple without noticing. Above all the idea of God as male has to be abandoned. That falsifies one's views of everything.

COMMENTARY

In this letter Shug expounds Alice Walker's own views on religion (see *The Same River Twice*, pp. 42–3, for example). Nettie says in Letter 86 that her faith has become less doctrinaire (see **Themes**, on **Religious belief**).

GLOSSARY
dime a coin worth ten cents
bangs fringes of hair

LETTER 74 (PAGE 169)

- Celie is to leave Albert.
- Women are taking charge.

From Celie to Nettie – Celie relates the story of Sofia, who is out of prison and restored to her family, although now almost a stranger to her children. Shug and Celie announce that they are going to Memphis, Tennessee. Celie denounces Albert for robbing her of Nettie: she is leaving him to 'enter into the Creation' (p. 170). Mary Agnes is leaving Harpo to go north as a singer. Sofia is called back to look after the mayor's family, but undertakes on her return to look after Harpo and his child by Mary Agnes, named Jolentha but known as Suzie Q. The women have taken charge.

LETTER 75 (PAGE 175)

- Hard words between Albert and Celie.

From Celie to Nettie – Shug, Celie, Mary Agnes and Grady are travelling to Memphis. Grady is now infatuated with Mary Agnes. Albert reacts badly to Celie's departure, heaping insults on her. In return she curses him: she threatens that everything will turn out badly for him until he recognises his crimes and decides to treat her properly.

COMMENTARY

This letter contains one of the most powerful dramatic scenes in the novel. Albert's denunciation of Celie, followed by her reply, 'I'm pore, I'm black … but I'm here' (p. 176), is the heart of the whole story. Celie seems to be possessed, as though by the spirit of her ancestors, so that a voice speaks through her when she stands up to Albert (see **Text 3** of **Extended commentaries** for a full discussion of this scene).

LETTER 76 (PAGE 177)

- Celie and Shug set up house together.

From Celie to Nettie – Shug owns a big house in Memphis, decorated throughout with figures and designs of elephants and turtles. The friends cook and listen to music. The newspapers show them how badly the world is being managed. Celie becomes obsessed with making pants. A few can be made for tolerable men, such as Odessa's husband Jack. Shug encourages her to start a business, selling brightly coloured pants to women everywhere.

LETTER 77 (PAGE 183)

- Celie runs 'Folkspants, Unlimited'.

From Celie to Nettie – Celie now has all she desires except the safe return of Nettie and the children. Her firm, 'Folkspants,

GLOSSARY

collards leaves of a cabbage-like vegetable

souse pigs' trotters and other parts, pickled

betsy bugs small insects

Unlimited a play on 'Limited Company'

CONTEXT

Like actual blues singers of this time, Shug uses her wealth to invest in business, but on Celie's behalf.

Unlimited', is prospering. She has two assistants, twins called Jerene and Darlene. Darlene is trying to teach her correct English. She tries to make Celie say 'we' rather than 'us' when Celie says 'us not so hot'. Celie is planning a pair of pants for Sofia with one leg red and the other purple.

LETTER 78 (PAGE 185)

- Sofia buries her mother.
- Sofia learns to smoke reefers.

From Celie to Nettie – Sofia's mother has died. Although pall-bearers at funerals have always been men, Sofia fights a successful battle against male prejudice, and she and her sisters carry the coffin to the grave. Celie is now much altered by Shug's influence: she teaches Harpo and Sofia how to smoke 'reefer'. Celie says that she takes the drug when she wants to talk to God or to make love. Sofia is shocked. They sit round the kitchen table and smoke reefers until they hear a mysterious humming, which may, perhaps, be the murmur of the universe.

LETTER 79 (PAGE 189)

- Albert learns to do housework.

From Celie to Nettie – Albert has reformed. He is now clean and hardworking, and even does housework and cooking. It seems that he deteriorated rapidly after Celie left him. He was rescued, however, by Harpo, who showed him great kindness. Harpo also made him return all Celie's remaining letters from Nettie, so lifting the effect of her curse.

LETTER 80 (PAGE 192)

- Nettie and Samuel marry in England.

From Nettie to Celie – Nettie is plump and grey-haired, and is now married to Samuel. The Olinka have been forced from their village by the rubber planters, and have to settle on a barren strip of land with no water supply for six months of the year. They suffer further indignity when they are reduced to buying tin to replace the sacred roofleaf. It is no surprise that they have lost whatever faith they may have had in missionaries. Nettie, Samuel and the children travel to England to seek help for the Olinka. On the journey, they meet the English lady who had been working as a missionary when they first arrived years before. She is returning to England to retire as she is now sixty-five, and she speaks of her early life in English upper-class society and how she sought escape from married life in England in missionary work. On arrival in England, Samuel and Nettie attend a meeting with a bishop whose only concern is the relationship between them now that Corrine is dead. He does not even consider the plight of the Olinka. Afterwards, Samuel talks of his doubts about their work, and reminisces about his early life with Corrine. He breaks down in tears, and in comforting him, Nettie reveals her love for him. They are married soon afterwards. Olivia reveals that Adam is unhappy in England because he misses Tashi. He is worried about her, as, in a gesture of support for traditional Olinka customs, she intends to undergo ritual facial scarring and circumcision. It seems clear that Adam loves Tashi.

COMMENTARY

Reference to 'a big war' (p. 194) is one of the hints to the novel's time-scheme. The year seems to be 1938 or 1939 (see **Narrative techniques**, on **Dating events**).

CHECK THE BOOK
See the novel *Arrow of God* (1964; revised 1974) by the Nigerian novelist Chinua Achebe for a very thoughtful fictional presentation of colonial problems.

LETTER 81 (PAGE 204)

LETTER 81 (PAGE 204)

- Nettie's family return to Africa.

QUESTION

If you could question Nettie about her time in Africa, what questions would you ask?

From Nettie to Celie – Nettie and Samuel have returned from England to the Olinka. Tashi has undergone the traditional initiation ceremonies, but has become ashamed of the marks on her face. Adam refuses to speak to her. He is desperate to return to America.

LETTER 82 (PAGE 206)

- Alphonso has died.

From Celie to Nettie – Alphonso's wife calls Celie to tell her that he is dead. The house and the business he ran were in fact owned by Celie's father, so they now belong to Celie and Nettie. Celie and Shug go to look at the house, and when they get there Celie finds Alphonso's tombstone which declares him to have been kind to the poor and helpless. Celie cannot believe that the beautiful house they find now belongs to her.

GLOSSARY

fortune cookies they have 'fortunes' written on thin slips of paper inserted before baking

flittish name fancy name

boocoos *(French)* correctly, beaucoup, a lot

LETTER 83 (PAGE 209)

- Shug finds a boyfriend.

From Celie to Nettie – Celie is broken-hearted because Shug has fallen in love with a young man called Germaine. Celie had spent the summer in Memphis working on the house she inherited in preparation for Nettie's arrival. When she returns, Shug talks eagerly about this nineteen-year-old, who plays the flute in her band, until Celie's evident grief checks her enthusiasm. She pleads for six months' grace: the affair cannot last longer than that. Celie grieves jealously nonetheless. Grady and Mary Agnes are growing marijuana in Panama.

LETTER 84 (PAGE 213)

- Celie is resentful about Shug's young man.
- Celie and Albert begin to be friends.

From Celie to Nettie – Sofia's youngest child (not Harpo's), Henrietta, is very ill. Caring for her helps to keep Celie from despair at Shug's infidelity. A diet of yams is prescribed, following African custom advocated by Nettie in a letter, but the child cannot stand the taste, so it has to be cunningly disguised. Celie and Albert draw closer together; talking about Shug is a bond between them. Albert proposes that they resume married life, but Celie speaks frankly, at last, of her physical repugnance at the sight of naked men.

LETTER 85 (PAGE 216)

- A telegram informs Celie that Nettie is dead.

From Celie to Nettie – an official telegram reports that Nettie and family are believed drowned after the ship bringing them from Africa was sunk by German mines. All Celie's letters to Nettie have, at the same time, been returned unopened.

COMMENTARY

The false telegraph shows the incompetence of people in authority. It also creates suspense in preparation for the happy ending in store.

> **CONTEXT**
>
> Britain, France and Canada declared war on Germany in September 1939; the United States joined the war in December 1941. German mines and U-boats (submarines) sank many ships in the Atlantic.

LETTER 86 (PAGE 217)

GLOSSARY

To Be or Not to Be
see *Hamlet*, Act III,
Scene 1, line 55

- Nettie hopes to return to America.

CONTEXT

Armed resistance
to colonial rule
preceded
independence in
some African
countries.

From Nettie to Celie – Tashi and her mother have run away to join a group of rebels against white rule, known as mbeles. The Olinka are falling sick because the destruction of their yam crops has removed their resistance to malaria. Nettie is full of worries and hopes about returning to America. She fears that Celie may be living in wretched conditions. She expects that life will be hard for her own family once they are back in the United States. But there will be much to discuss, says Nettie, always a teacher, including her evolving conception of God. Africa has taught her to think of God as a Spirit unconstrained by the images of one religion or another, to be seen in Christ or in roofleaf. The letter ends with the dramatic news that Adam has gone away in search of Tashi.

COMMENTARY

The reference to thirty years having passed since the sisters were last together is another useful clue to the time-scheme. The date seems to be 1940 or 1941 (see **Narrative techniques**, on **Dating events**).

LETTER 87 (PAGE 220)

GLOSSARY

the trees with you
God be with you!
(since Shug has taught
her that God is present
in nature)

cotton gin a machine
to separate seeds and
other impurities from
cotton; a symbol of
white oppression of
black people

- Love of Shug acts as a bond between Celie and Albert.

Celie to Nettie – Celie stands naked before her mirror, contemplating the changes brought by the years, because she is afraid that Shug no longer loves her. Shug and Germaine are touring the country. Albert, although still known to Celie only as Mr —, is now her only friend at hand. She finds that in spite of all the wrongs he has done her she cannot hate him. He has reformed, and he too loves Shug. He protects Celie from the unwanted attentions of men Sofia and Harpo put in her way. Celie and Albert sit and reminisce about earlier events in their lives together.

Sofia still has troubles. Miss Eleanor Jane, the mayor's daughter brought up by Sofia, is still devoted to her. Eleanor Jane keeps visiting Sofia, bringing her husband and baby and demanding admiration. Sofia would prefer to be left alone. After her sufferings she cannot accept this white woman as a friend, and she is too honest to pretend to feel warmth towards the baby. Other black women pretend, she tells Eleanor Jane, because they are afraid of whites.

Shug writes, describing her travels. Celie is angry with her, but tries to accept Shug's right to her own life. She and Albert talk about Shug. Albert says she is 'manly', but Celie thinks that her virtues are womanly. They also talk about pants, symbolic, they agree, of freedom and power in modern America. Celie tells him how men wear robes in Africa. Civilisation there is profoundly different in other ways. Africans believe that the first man was black and created long before Adam. The Olinka, she has heard from Nettie, worship the snake. Albert finds her good company.

COMMENTARY

Celie's explanation of how African myth differs from the Bible story of Adam and Eve is another stage in her rejection of the fundamentalist beliefs of her early life.

> **GLOSSARY (cont)**
> **adobe** Shug describes a house made of sun-dried brick of clay and straw
> **a scanless** scandalously
> **Omatangu** the first man, in African myth

 CHECK THE BOOK
For the Bible story of Adam and Eve, their nakedness, the tempting of Eve by the Serpent, and their expulsion from the garden, see Genesis 2–3.

LETTER 88 (PAGE 234)

- Adam marries Tashi.
- The family leave Africa.

From Nettie to Celie – Adam has brought Tashi home, protesting, from the rebels' camp. He caught up with and accompanied her and her mother to the mbeles' encampment. He persuaded them to return with him. Tashi is afraid to marry Adam because she thinks Americans will despise her. But Adam has his face marked with carvings like hers: he has become Adam Omatangu, Adam of Africa. Samuel then marries Adam and Tashi, and the whole family set out for the coast to find a ship bound for home.

LETTER 89 (PAGE 237)

- Celie has Shug at home with her and dreams that Nettie may still be alive.

From Celie to Nettie – Shug has been trying to get news of Nettie from the State Department, but the men there are racialists and unco-operative. Celie has not lost hope that Nettie may be alive. Sofia is working in the store which Celie and Nettie have inherited. She scares the white man hired in Alphonso's time. Eleanor Jane is caring for Henrietta. She has at long last found out the circumstances in which Sofia went to work for her family. Sofia thinks there is hope for Eleanor Jane yet. Albert sits on his veranda, sewing. He is designing a shirt to match Celie's pants. Shug's return home makes Celie happy, for the moment. Shug explains that Germaine has been sent away to college. Celie tells her that she has been spending time with Albert, mentioning him by name for the first time.

COMMENTARY

Celie's use of Albert's name, here and in the next letter, reflects her acceptance of him as a friend, although not as a husband. He seems to have changed, in these final letters (see **Characterisation** on **Albert/Mr. —**).

LETTER 90 (PAGE 242)

- Happy ending

'Dear God ... Dear Everything' (p. 242), Celie writes. Nettie and the children are home, to the happiest of reunions. Even Albert is included, as he counts now as 'family'. Mary Agnes has left Grady, and returned from Panama to look after Suzie Q. Tashi and Adam are admired by all. Celie knows that the young people think that she and her friends are old, but she thinks 'this the youngest us ever felt' (p. 244).

COMMENTARY

Celie announces that she has stopped writing to God in Letter 73. Now she addresses him again, but with a new understanding of what he means to her. The final 'Amen' [So be it!] is a thankful one (see **Themes**, on **Religious belief**).

EXTENDED COMMENTARIES

TEXT 1   (PAGES 42–5)

From:

> 'They git halfway up the step, Mr. — look up at me. Celie, he say. This here Shug Avery.'

To:

> 'I wash her body, it feel like I'm praying. My hands tremble and my breath short.'

Shug Avery's first appearance, sick but too evil to die, is a good example of how vivid and dramatic Celie's terse narrative style can be.

We are accustomed by now to Celie's relating of past events in the present tense and her frequent omission of words and **morphemes** that act as grammatical markers. We may not notice, therefore, how effectively her habits of speech give these scenes qualities of immediacy and urgency for which literary devices such as **ellipsis** or the **historic present tense** are used elsewhere. Omission of the verb 'to be', for example, makes the sentences about Harpo and Sofia at the end of the first paragraph seem like stage directions preceding some piece of dramatic action. In the phrases describing Shug as Celie first sees her, removal of the verbs is reminiscent of the technique of **stream of consciousness** where ellipsis suggests the flow of a character's thoughts and sense impressions. It also lets us hear Celie's speaking voice: 'But he there'. Omission of grammatical markers also gives a freshness to everyday phraseology.

QUESTION

'Nettie is an earnest character and Alice Walker is in earnest in the letters from Africa, but most of the drama and life of the novel is in Celie's letters.' Do you agree? Explain why.

CHECK THE BOOK

See Virginia Woolf's novel *The Waves* (1941), for an example of the technique of 'stream of consciousness'.

These are features of Celie's speech. Typographical simplifications are effective, too. Dispensing with quotation marks and the convention of a new line for a new speaker produces a sense of intimacy, as Albert's and Shug's voices interrupt Celie's without formality: 'She too evil for that. Turn loose my goddam hand, she say'.

This first meeting with Shug is a turning point in Celie's life. Hitherto Celie has known Shug from a photograph and has found sisterly reassurance in her eyes. Now it is the eyes that command attention. Though feverish, they look 'mean', ready to kill a snake and not scotch it. A more evocative term still is used twice. Shug is 'more evil than my mama' and that is what keeps her alive. She is too evil to let Albert hold her hand. This sort of evil is obviously not the usual sense of moral depravity to be seen, for example, in Alphonso. It indicates malice, as in 'an evil temper' (sometimes said of a horse), but also has a broad range of positive meaning when applied to Shug. It implies vitality (she is hard to kill), feistiness, spunk, and independence of all the world, especially men. It is the opposite of the meekness gone soft (for Nettie can be dignified in her meekness) found in women like Celie whose spirit has been crushed, or in Albert when he acts like a weak little boy. Albert's last words may be true, but she is willing to stand against the world.

QUESTION

Choose a scene that seems especially effective and discuss it in detail, explaining its place in the design of the novel.

This helps to explain why Shug so fascinates Celie, possessing in abundance the qualities Celie lacks and needs. But the passage makes explicit what must be grasped in interpreting the whole novel, that Celie is possessed by sexual passion for the other woman. Shug's nakedness, black and lean and to Celie astonishing, her decisiveness ('You sure *is* ugly'), her humour and theatricality (hand on hip), the charisma which makes her a great blues queen, all together captivate Celie and she falls in love for good. Sweetness, too, plays a part in the charisma, accounting for her name (short for 'sugar'). Sisterhood, the novel asserts, can be the conventional bond uniting Celie and Nettie, or the solidarity between Mary Agnes and Sofia, or homosexual love, whatever **patriarchy** may have to say.

The passage also deepens the interest of Albert. Shared love of Shug will eventually reconcile Albert and Celie, though only after the love and inspiration of Shug have allowed her to rebel against him, so it is fitting that Celie should remember Albert's name and allow herself to say it here. She is usually too frightened to name him at all. Albert's devotion, even at the cost of drink and tobacco, brings out the stronger will and personality of Shug, but also reminds us that his brutal treatment of Celie is not the whole guide to his nature. The Albert of the novel differs sharply in this respect from his counterpart in the film.

CHECK THE BOOK
For Walker's comments on Albert, see the essay 'In the Closet of the Soul', in *Living by the Word*.

We see here what an artist with words Alice Walker has made Celie and how her powers of self-expression develop as she matures. Love brings out her delight in language:

> First time I got the full sight of Shug Avery long black body with it black plum nipples look like her mouth, I thought I had turned into a man.
> What you staring at? she ast. Hateful. She weak as a kitten. But her mouth just pack with claws. (p. 45)

Imagery such as 'mouth just pack [packed] with claws' (catty in her speech) arises from the poet in Celie. A little later she says, of Shug, 'she smile, like a razor opening' (p. 51). The **alliteration** of 'b' and 'p' and 'l' in 'long black body with it black plum nipples' would have pleased D. H. Lawrence.

The novel celebrates the creativity of women, especially in music and design. Celie later regrets that she can't cook well. She constantly shows us how well she can write.

·TEXT 2 (PAGES 131–3)·

From:

> 'Looking over the heads of the children at the end of this tale, I saw coming slowly towards us, a large brown spiky thing as big as a room, with a dozen legs walking slowly and carefully under it.'

To:

> 'For some reason all of her bites turn into deep, runny sores, and she has a lot of trouble sleeping at night because the noises from the forest frighten her.'

Writing to Celie, soon after her arrival in Africa, Nettie describes a village ceremony and gives an outline of her daily routine.

In Nettie's letters, Alice Walker perfectly captures the style and tone of a missionary magazine of the period, careful, earnest and unassuming. All Africa and her prodigies are recorded in much the same manner, gods and insect bites alike. The correct school-teacher's prose counterbalances the non-standard discourse of Celie's letters. Nettie's are carefully composed pieces of writing, produced at leisure. In her sister's letters, which sometimes sound as urgent as dispatches from a battle, we hear the rhythms of live speech. Although Celie's style is much more fun, Nettie's writing has its own dignity and appeal, connected with the disciplined regularity of the way of life described in this passage.

The writing is functional and makes its points clear. These often serve to interweave themes shared by the African and American parts of the story. The ceremony of delivering the roof is part of the villagers' welcome when Samuel, Corrine, Nettie and the children arrive at their African mission station. A villager has just told the Olinka tale, related by Nettie, of a greedy chief who used land assigned to the sacred roofleaf for his own private cultivation. The ritual of honouring a new roof is preserved among the people as a mark of reverence for the leaf itself. Here, in a surprising shape, is an African God. Yet Celie will not be completely surprised when she reads about it because Shug has been teaching her to see the divine in trees and in all of nature rather than in the **patriarchal** images of Christianity.

CHECK THE BOOK

For vivid scenes of old village life and traditional religion in a Nigerian novel, see Chinua Achebe, *Things Fall Apart* (1958).

The next letter reveals another connection, in the theme of education for girls. Nettie regrets the backwardness of the Olinka men, and Olinka women who submit to their prejudices, wherever this impedes female emancipation. For example, the villagers send boys to school but not girls. A comparison with America is spotted by the child Olivia, who makes it without hesitation: 'They're like white people at home who don't want colored people to learn'. When she sets out to educate her friend Tashi, the image of the two girls, American and African, sharing knowledge in secret under the sheltering roofleaf, in defiance of men, attractively reaffirms the theme of worldwide sisterhood.

It may occur to some readers, especially if they have read African novels about colonial encounters with traditional culture, that Nettie does not try to analyse the problems with any depth or subtlety. But this limitation (if we feel it) does not interfere with the novel's long-range, transatlantic overview of colonial Africa, or with its plain polemical purposes. Nettie reveals the problems, the indifference of the rubber company which obliterates the rooftree and offers tin-roofed huts in exchange, the remoteness of the church authorities in England, and at least one barbarity to be found in Africa, the female genital mutilation (female circumcision) which Alice Walker has described and condemned elsewhere (see **Background,** on **Other works by Alice Walker**).

CHECK
THE BOOK
See 'Heaven
Belongs to You' in
*Anything We Love
Can Be Saved* for
Walker's campaign
against female
genital mutilation.

Instead of solutions, Nettie offers emotions, including indignation and concern, but mostly an unyielding love, which is given to the children and in due course to Samuel, but is concentrated on her sister. 'Dear Celie … always, no matter what I'm doing, I am writing to you', 'Dear Nettie' – these forms of address resound with the devotion that unites the two sisters. It is this bond of sisterhood, so strongly felt, shared by Shug, Sofia, Mary Agnes, Tashi and Olivia, rather than social or political analysis, that conveys the novel's hope for the future.

TEXT 3 (PAGES 175–6)

From:

'Dear Nettie,
Well, you know wherever there's a man, there's trouble.'

To:

'Amen, say Shug. Amen, amen.'

Celie is leaving Albert to live in Memphis with Shug. In the previous letter she reports how she rebelled against Albert, saying it is time 'to leave you and enter into the Creation' (p. 170). Now, it seems the Creation curses him through her lips.

Shug has persuaded Celie that trees, or anything in nature, can serve as a better image of God than a man, especially a white man. The words of her curses now come to her as though 'from the trees'. Perhaps it is her guardian 'Familiar' who speaks, or a long-repressed rage which finds utterance while she is for a few moments 'beside herself'.

CHECK THE FILM
Spielberg's film weakens Albert's lines at this point by omitting 'Goddam'.

The curses are not especially forceful in phraseology, but they are appropriate and the drama of the scene lends them strength. Albert's resistance adds to the drama. He speaks with remarkable conviction: 'Look at you. You black, you pore, you ugly, you a woman. Goddam, he say, you nothing at all'. 'Goddam' is the word Albert pauses on in feigned surprise at just what a nothing Celie is. 'Goddam' is spoken on a rising note bringing the heavy stresses on 'black', 'pore', 'ugly', 'woman' to a climax, before the dismissive falling cadence in 'you nothing at all'. Albert may be a weak man but he has a good ear for effective sentence rhythm and Celie echoes him in her final, victorious assertion, ending 'But I'm here'.

This is a crucial passage. Celie *is* here, although Albert cannot yet acknowledge her because his contempt for the concept of 'poor black ugly woman' obstructs his awareness of the person he married. The conviction Walker gets into his words serves her purpose because it shows how instinctive his contempt is. She wants the reader to believe that all men, Olinka, American, black and white, share this unthinking assumption that a woman is inferior. She mentions with approval the remark of her friend Dennis Banks that 'there is a little bit of Mister in all of us' (*The Same River Twice*, p. 36).

This is the most powerful of all the encounters between Albert and Celie: it demonstrates very forcefully the lightly spoken ironic reversal of a common sexist saying ('Where there's a woman, there's trouble') which opens the letter. That little bit of Mister means trouble.

CHECK THE BOOK
Walker's *By the Light of My Father's Smile* uses 'Ho!', an African equivalent to 'So be it!', in a way reminiscent of 'Amen' in this novel.

'Amen', meaning 'so be it', the traditional close to a Christian prayer, becomes the closing word of Celie's letters (and of the book) when she stops writing to God, in the letter where Shug speaks about the divine Spirit present everywhere, and writes to Nettie instead (pp. 164–8). Shug is allowed the last word in the present crucial letter, which proclaims that not all the male contempt in the world can reduce Celie to 'nothing at all'. 'But I'm here,' she says, and Shug says 'Amen', three times. Walker means it to be a sacred affirmation.

CRITICAL APPROACHES

CHARACTERISATION

Alice Walker thinks of her characters as people. Creative writing for her is a process of discovery rather than invention. Her brief afterword says 'I thank everyone in this book for coming', and she has described the experience of waiting for her characters to make themselves known to her (see *In Search of Our Mothers' Gardens*, pp. 355–60). This is, perhaps, a writer's rather than a reader's way of thinking about character, but it does indicate how vividly Walker's people live in her mind.

One practical way to think about characters is to consider how they have been or might be interpreted by actors in a stage or screen adaptation. It is interesting to read Walker's notes on the characters made when she was hoping to influence Steven Spielberg's casting. She stresses physical features and postures which reflect inner states: Celie cowers in the early scenes but later when she begins 'to strut' (as Celie says, p. 126) she looks more herself and grows beautiful. Albert is small in body and mind, while Sofia is stout in body and personality (see *The Same River Twice*, pp. 51–4).

Characters often refer to aspects of their early lives that help to explain them. Sofia and Shug both tell Celie that they grew to be strong and sometimes aggressive by reacting against early pressures at home. Harpo has been indoctrinated by his father into his belief, disastrous in his marriage to Sofia, that women must be kept in order. Albert's weakness goes back to having been dominated by his own father. Celie spends the whole novel outgrowing the exceptionally crippling experiences of her early life.

The novel teaches us that characters can change for the better under the influence of love. Celie matures through love of Shug. Albert is saved by his love for Shug from the narrow and embittering misogyny which so degrades the character of Alphonso. By the end

CONTEXT

Some feminists would dismiss this idea of 'male/female elements'.

of the story this has enabled him to grasp that Celie loves her too and they become friends.

It is sometimes suggested that a male element in a woman's character or a womanly element in a man's can be a source of strength. Celie notices that 'Shug talk and act sometimes like a man' (p. 72). Sofia takes to 'manly' activities, including outside heavy work, while Harpo enjoys child-minding and cooking. These two characters display Walker's belief that **gender** is distinct from sexual identity, and that the roles socially assigned to men and women can be destructive if they are rigidly enforced.

One technique in creating fictional characters is naming them. Shug is felt to be apter than Lillie: when she sings or makes love she is sweet as sugar. It may be that **phonaesthemic** associations with 'shush' and 'shucks' and 'shrug' and 'hug' as well as with 'sugar' ('She just so sweet they call her Shug', p. 103) give this name its strong evocative influence on our idea of what the character is like. 'Squeak' has a different and more dignified role, as a singer rather than just a little 'yellow' bargirl, when she is called Mary Agnes, and she tends to insist on her proper name. Sometimes a name is symbolic. Walker mentions that Sofia 'is named after the goddess of wisdom' (*The Same River Twice*, p. 41). How characters name or fail to name one another is also telling. It is not until the end that Celie can say 'Albert'.

CONTEXT

Holy Wisdom (*Sophia*) also has a place in Christian tradition.

Attention should also be paid, when considering character, to the voices created to bring them alive: to Shug's emphatic forms of the verb 'to be': 'it *bees* that way' (p. 10) and 'You sure *is* ugly' (p. 42), to Albert's 'Goddam' and to many other vividly individual habits of speech.

CELIE

'I have always been a good girl' (page 3), Celie tells God in the novel's first line. She grows in the course of the story from the pitiful child of the opening pages to the sensible, happy woman of the last. Although always vulnerable, she is steadfast; although often abused, she is loving; when loved, she is able to respond and grow. It is difficult to create a good and attractive character in fiction, especially when the character tells his or her own story; Walker succeeds with Celie.

Celie is meant to be more than a credible portrait of a good woman, however. Walker has aimed to present a process of emancipation of a woman, body and soul, from the domination of men. At first, Celie is almost entirely in the power of Alphonso and Albert. She grows to be wholly independent of men. The idea of a free woman, conceived this way, is more radical and feminist than the traditional idea of a good wife and mother, but in this portrayal goodness and emancipation go together, and the novelist's success with the character supports the controversial arguments she puts forward.

Even as an unhappy waif writing to God because nobody else pays attention, the child Celie is not without dignity. The strength of Walker's art here is in its freedom from sentimentality. Raped, beaten, deprived of her babies and of her mother, Celie retains a genuine innocence and courage: 'I see him looking at my little sister. She scared. But I say I'll take care of you. With God help' (p. 5). 'I'll take care' is effectively restrained, in the appalling circumstances, and God is a familiar, trusted presence in these early pages. There is poignancy in Celie's 'dressing trampy' (p. 9) to lure Pa away from Nettie, and in the scene of her efforts on her wedding night to clean and control Albert's children, her head bleeding from a stone Harpo threw. However brutal those who rule over Celie, they cannot brutalise her. Walker shows the resilience and good nature of her heroine in these and many other sensitively written scenes in the early letters. They include Celie's meeting with Corrine in the store, in Letter 10, and her receipt of the surly confidences of the love-stricken teenaged Harpo, in Letter 13. (For more on the effective restraint of Celie's style of expression, see **Language and style**).

CHECK THE BOOK
See the early chapters of *Pamela* (1740) by Samuel Richardson for a heroine who protests too much about her own virtue (in another **epistolary** novel).

Walker does not make the mistake of early novelists who tried to persuade us their heroines were perfect. When she makes Celie advise Harpo to beat Sofia, this reflects the fact of life that the oppressed tend to accept the thinking of those who oppress them. It also avoids the danger of making Celie too good to be true. She is not a saint: she has resented Sofia's pitying glances. We know Harpo is sure to get the worst of a fight with Sofia, so we do not

disapprove too much of Celie's disloyalty. Her conscience also
exacts a penance in the form of insomnia.

? QUESTION

Discuss the novel's
presentation of
religious faith.

Two relationships dominate Celie's life. Her love for Nettie is more
of a bond because of their desperate need for mutual support in the
early years. Love of Nettie is connected with love of God, in Celie's
mind. She breaks off the letters to him because she decides that
writing to her sister is enough, in Letter 73. Nothing can diminish
the strength of this sisterly bond. It nourishes Celie's unyielding
quality and her gentler virtues. Her other great passion, for Shug
Avery, is very different.

Celie is sexually attracted to women, and not to men. She tells us in
Letter 5 that she looks at women because she is not afraid of them.
She tells Albert in Letter 84 that naked men look to her 'like frogs'.
She scarcely notices and does not tell us that Albert is a handsome
man, as we learn from Corrine in Letter 10; she finds no sexual
pleasure or satisfaction in marriage. Some readers may think that
early abuse has killed her heterosexuality. Others may think she
may have been born homosexual. However it may be, Shug
captivates Celie from the first glimpse, in a photograph (Letter 6).
Dressed to kill, full of devilry, beauty and glamour, Shug is all she
does not hope to be herself. This Shug of the photograph occupies
Celie's fantasies. At a bad moment she looks at Shug's eyes in the
picture and reads there words of sympathy: 'Yeah, it *bees* that way
sometimes' (Letter 7). Shug's presence in the neighbourhood thrills
Celie, in Letter 14; and a dream seems to have come true (as often
happens in this novel) when she becomes Shug's nurse (Letter 24).
The strong sexual attraction is announced without fuss. Looking at
Shug's body, Celie feels that she herself must have 'turned into a
man' (p. 45). Shug's dedication of a song to her is a proud moment,
in Letter 33. It is in Letter 35 that Shug begins to teach her about
sexual pleasure, but it is not until twelve letters and many years later
that they make love on a night when Albert and Grady are out
drinking.

The two attachments of her life are now connected, since Shug the
lover promptly discovers Nettie the missing sister by noticing the
letters with 'funny' stamps on them (Letter 50). Rage at Albert's

theft combines with confidence drawn from her lover, and she starts to act independently. One turning point is Letter 67, where she learns that Alphonso is not her father or Nettie's, and another is Letter 74, where she tells Albert that he is a 'lowdown dog'.

Celie wins many kinds of freedom. She abandons her false picture of God as an old white man in favour of a Walkerian belief in the Spirit that unites our inner life with the universe. She comes to see God in the mystery of how nature is, for example in the colour purple. With this new creed comes her acceptance of sexual pleasure. 'Folkspants, Unlimited', her business venture, makes her financially independent. Some readers may suspect it is Celie's money, partly derived from Folkspants, that enables her to chat with Albert in the last chapters, as an equal of sorts. By the end she has come to accept that Shug is a free spirit who will lead her own life, with male lovers as well as with her. By the time of the last letter she deserves her happy ending.

> **CONTEXT**
>
> The stamps appear 'funny' only because they are not American. Even Shug is unaccustomed to letters from abroad.

SHUG AVERY

Shug is as remarkable as the story requires. Her parents called her Lillie but she turned out to be (to all her admirers) the queen Honeybee, or Sugar, or Shug. 'She just so sweet they call her Shug', Celie says (p. 103). ['Shug' was the nickname of Alice Walker's Aunt Malsenior – who gave the novelist her second forename.] She can be sweet when performing as a professional blues singer. At other times, as Celie says, 'her mouth just pack with claws' (p. 45). She succeeds as a singer, and so gets rich, because she can dominate an audience, and she dominates her lovers, too. It may have been rebellion against her strange mother, who loathed all physical contact with others (p. 103), that made her sensual, independent and strong-willed. She sometimes surprises herself by how ruthless she can be, as we notice when she tells Celie how cruel she was to Aunt Julie when this unlucky woman was made to marry Albert: 'I was so mean, and so wild' (p. 104). She loves Albert because he is so 'funny' and 'little', and because he could make her laugh in the old days, but she has never wanted to marry him – only to make sure he prefers her to all other women. She marries the foolish, toothy Grady, and pays for his car while ordering him about, as she orders Albert, and later spends a few months with the attractive nineteen-

year-old Germaine, who pleases her for a while. She loves men with
passion, as she often says, but does not intend to be subject to any
man. It may be that she has a 'masculine element' in her nature.
Celie observes that she often speaks like a man, especially when
commenting on women (p. 72). She is kind to Celie, staying on at
Albert's to make sure he stops beating her, and to Mary Agnes, helping
her become a singer, but she enjoys her power over them both.

She is a free spirit in every realm. Celie thinks her too 'evil' to
submit to illness for long (p. 43). She is too restless to stay long at
home with anyone – to the regret of Celie and Albert. She has a
good, opinionated mind, and seems to have thought out her own
unorthodox views (many shared with Alice Walker). She takes her
bisexual nature for granted and enjoys it. She is free of the fear of
God, although she checks Celie's blasphemous talk in Letter 73.
Some of her religious notions are vague, but she is quite sure God is
not male. She sounds almost facetious when she speaks the lines in
Letter 73 that give the novel its title (p. 167). It could be said that
she is serious about God but not about the solemn religious terms
devised by men.

**CHECK
THE BOOK**
See the first essay in
*Anything We Love
can Be Saved* for
Walker's views on
religion.

Where many characters are strictly regional figures, who think of
Memphis as a great city, Shug is at home everywhere. In creating
her, Alice Walker had in mind the great women blues singers,
including Bessie Smith (said in Letter 33 to have been a friend of
Shug's). Some readers may regret that we do not hear more about
the people Shug must have known in California and New York.
(For more on Bessie Smith and the blues, see **Symbolism: Song** and
Historical background.)

ALBERT/MR —

Albert is known to Celie as 'Mr —' until the final letter, when she
accepts him as 'family', although not as a husband. It is not until the
end of Letter 89 that she acknowledges his name. Like Alphonso,
and, it is implied, all men in this community, he lacks any respect
for women. He looks on his second marriage as the acquisition of
two pieces of property, Celie and a cow, the latter being the greater
asset. The beatings and insults he inflicts on Celie combined with
his indifference to his children, and his idleness, make him

despicable. He is a fairly sensual man, callous and childishly petulant, as Shug tells him, but oddly stubborn in hiding Nettie's letters for so many years. (It could be argued that this **melodramatic** aspect of his role does not fit him: he would have destroyed the letters.) He is fundamentally weak, as some bullies are; he beats Celie because 'she isn't Shug', until Shug makes him stop; he suffers a nervous breakdown when Celie leaves him.

There is another Albert, however. He was loved by Shug in their youth, for his laughter and his dancing, and he has loved Shug ever since. He takes her in when she is sick and in disgrace and grieves over her. Love of Shug gives him feelings in common with Celie, and he begins to be a more attractive character from that point on. But he is only allowed a degree of sympathy. By hiding the letters he earns Celie's term of abuse: he is 'a lowdown dog' (p. 170). In the next letter (75) he speaks the anti-womanist manifesto at the novel's heart: 'You black, you pore, you ugly, you a woman. Goddam, you nothing at all' (p. 176).

He appears strangely transformed in the last letters, after his breakdown, sewing pants and talking sensibly. This is partly explicable if his new respect for Celie is based on her newly acquired wealth. But some readers may doubt whether all aspects of this character's behaviour fit together.

SOFIA

Sofia is a contrast to Celie. A brutal upbringing has made her a fighter. She has had to fight off her father, brother and cousins: 'A girl child ain't safe in a family of men' (p. 38). Big and strong, she and her sisters learnt to hit back, and Sofia now does so as a reflex action. When Harpo tries to beat her she batters him. She knocks down Mary Agnes when slapped by this smaller girl; and she knocks down the white mayor when he slaps her. The police compel her to submit to beatings and to the prison regime for the first three years of her twelve-year sentence, and then to the humiliating condition of a prisoner-maid, a kind of slavery, in the mayor's household. In spite of all this ill-treatment, she remains a formidable woman when released.

CHECK THE FILM

Spielberg's Albert remains an unsympathetic character almost to the end, a fault in the film, according to Walker.

QUESTION

How might Albert defend his treatment of Celie and explain the failure of his marriage?

Sofia is very strong-minded, instinctively rejecting all the traditional ideas about a woman's role. She takes naturally to 'manly' activities, including heavy outdoor work. Far from 'minding' [obeying] Harpo, she takes all domestic decisions, such as when to take the children to visit her sisters. If only Harpo would forget about trying to rule her, it seems they might be well-matched in a marriage free from conventional roles, because he likes cooking and caring for children. When she leaves Harpo, however, she chooses a man who looks like a prize-fighter; it is not clear how we are to interpret that.

Sofia is a character who sometimes plays a comic role, but suffers a tragic fate. We may be amused when Harpo talks about his injuries from the barn-door and cantankerous mule; but when we hear, in Celie's recounting of Sofia's downfall, that the mayor has slapped her, we share Mary Agnes's horror at what is going to happen next to this woman of fighting spirit, in a society such as hers. That she survives her sufferings and imprisonment, and ends the novel as a dignified and courageous woman, is a symbol of the triumph of good over evil.

MARY AGNES/'SQUEAK'

CONTEXT

Mary Agnes's tour of the North is a reminder of the nationwide popularity of the blues.

Mary Agnes is foremost among the minor female characters. Although as Mary Agnes she gains in dignity, she seems to relapse somewhat in Grady's company, but at the end of the story she is independent once more, preparing to tour the north of the country with her new songs. She contributes to the theme of solidarity among women, in her instant concern when Sofia is arrested, and in helping to look after Sofia's children later on.

HARPO

We often sympathise with Harpo. He is to be pitied when he relives the occasion of his mother's murder in a nightmare (p. 28). We may sympathise, too, when Sofia and their children leave him. We may admire him when he rescues Albert from despair; the sight of him asleep and 'holding his daddy in his arms' makes Sofia start to 'feel again for Harpo' (p. 191). He is attractive in a different way when he recovers his spirits after Sofia's departure and sets up his jukejoint.

At other times, Harpo is a farcical figure of fun: eating six eggs for breakfast, for example, in his effort to become as big and powerful as Sofia (pp. 53–5).

ALPHONSO

Alphonso remarks that May Ellen, a teenage girl when he marries her after the death of Celie's mother, has left him because she 'Got too old for me I reckon' (p. 154). Her replacement is another child-wife called Daisy. He rapes Celie when she is fourteen and soon afterwards has his eye on the still younger Nettie. He particularly enjoys treating these girls as slaves. Celie is made to cut his hair just before and immediately after his violation of her. Alphonso parades her before Albert and speaks of her as though a slave for sale: 'she ain't fresh' (p. 9). He deliberately conceals the facts of their parentage from Celie and Nettie, and says in defence that knowledge of their father's fate would have upset them. He also withholds their property. 'Pa' is the least attractive of the characters.

GRADY

In Alice Walker's novels, men are (in general) the weaker sex, although not the gentler. Albert, Harpo, Alphonso and Grady exemplify male weakness and male impulses to bully. Like Harpo, Grady is to be seen as a thoughtless man who repeats unthinkingly the opinions of others. His red braces and bow ties look vulgar to Celie (because she is jealous of him). To end his days growing marijuana in Panama seems an appropriate fate for him (although not for Mary Agnes who leaves him there and returns to sing and look after her daughter).

CHECK THE FILM

Costume in Spielberg's film repays careful attention (although it sometimes differs from clothing in the novel).

SAMUEL AND ADAM

The Reverend Samuel and his son Adam are exceptional members of the novel's cast: they are reasonably intelligent and sensible men, and they have a positive attitude towards women. We see and hear very little of them, however, and then only through the medium of Nettie's letters. She praises Samuel first as a protector and later as a husband; she praises Adam first as a pleasant boy, later as a principled young man and the lover of Tashi; but she does not attempt the kind of dialogue and action that bring Albert and Harpo to life in Celie's letters.

NETTIE, CORRINE AND THE CHILDREN

Nettie has all the good qualities necessary for a missionary, a school-teacher and a maiden aunt. She is a conscientious girl at school. She remains dutiful and earnest throughout the story. She also has enough tact to survive in her awkward situation in Samuel's family without losing his respect or the love of the children. She shares with Celie an unusual amount of stamina. Her letters reveal a thoughtful view of the African scene, appropriately prim but also rightly indignant, especially in condemning the faults of colonial rule.

We are bound to take Nettie's side, but we may also feel sorry for Corrine, whose jealousy is understandable and whose death is required by the story (since another good man for Nettie to marry might be hard to find). Nettie and Corrine have taught Olivia the progressive, liberal American views which Olivia passes on to Tashi. Tashi's difficulties, placed between the missionaries and her own people, are outlined in Nettie's letters, but remain in the distant background of the story.

THEMES

SLAVERY

CONTEXT

In 1865 the 13th Amendment to the Constitution freed all slaves; the 14th Amendment, a year later, granted citizenship to former slaves.

Although slavery was abolished in the United States in 1865, habits of mind formed under slavery continued to degrade human relations, as the novel constantly shows. 'Girl' as a form of address (p. 76) and 'boy' meaning a servant (p. 155) are terms that date back to the era of slavery. They are still in use because the mentality has not changed. Alphonso and Albert treat women like slaves, and this is reflected in their speech: 'I can let you have Celie', 'I got a fresh one in there myself' (p. 9). The scene where Mr —, on his horse, inspects Celie, who is made to turn about in front of him, is meant to remind us of the purchase of a slave.

Miss Millie, the mayor's wife, treats Sofia as a slave, and so provokes her indignant reply, which leads to the mayor's intervention and

Sofia's arrest, beating and imprisonment. It is even implied that Sofia is treated worse as a 'free' woman, when in prison, than she is when she is, in effect, the 'slave' looking after Miss Millie's children.

The theme of slavery links the African part of the story to the American. Nettie's letters express the strongest feelings for the home continent, from which the ancestors of African-Americans were brought by European slave traders (pp. 114–15, for example). She is angry, however, when the Olinka refuse to discuss the slave trade (p. 140), because they are trying to hide the fact that Africans were responsible for selling slaves to European traders.

In America and in Africa, the novel insists, the inability of men to see women as equals is akin to the old slave-owning mentality, which is far from having been eradicated from the world.

> **CONTEXT**
>
> Slave markets remained, in some parts of Africa, even in the period of the novel.

FEMINISM

Feminism is the customary term, but we should bear in mind that Alice Walker prefers the term 'womanist' for a black feminist – commenting that 'womanist is to feminist as purple is to lavender', darker and stronger too. Walker's purpose is to show the ill treatment black women have endured, especially in the early twentieth century, in the southern United States and also in Africa, and to show how they have struggled to free themselves.

The injustice of white supremacy in the old South is forcefully demonstrated, especially in the sufferings of Sofia, but more space and emphasis are given to men's injustice to women, regardless of race, and to the gumption of the women who rebel. In contrast to the victims of male brutality, Shug Avery is a heroic figure, in Celie's eyes, deserving the colour purple, because she has won her independence and will not be any man's 'mule'. She lives as she sings, boldly; and is indifferent to 'how people talk' – that is, to the prejudiced gossip and slander of a **patriarchal** society. Like Sofia she has learnt to fight, but more effectively, without using fists, and she teaches Celie to do the same.

The theme of emancipation is present throughout the novel. Celie and Nettie progress from a state of near-slavery to independence and the power of self-expression: Nettie as a wife and teacher, Celie as a clothes-designer and business woman, needing no husband. The novel asserts that all women are sisters. Comforted and strengthened by Shug, Celie is ready to fight Albert when the discovery of the letters reveals the depth of his guilt. Only Shug can then restrain her – meek though she has been until now – from killing him. When she first curses and then leaves Albert, Shug gives her a home in Memphis and helps her to launch her own business. The scene described in Letter 74 shows Celie, Shug, Sofia and Mary Agnes (who has already proved her sisterhood with Sofia), uniting to assert their independence from the men.

MEN

Men are seen at their worst in this feminist novel. There is a background chorus of male grumbling about the inferiority of the sex they assume to be weaker. The chorus is largely composed of buffoons such as Alphonso, Harpo and the white mayor. Harpo has been taught his privileged position in life (and, it seems, little else): 'Women work, I'm a man', he says while still a boy and asked by Albert's sister Kate to do some chores (Letter 12). Albert teaches Harpo that women have to be beaten because they are like children; but men are the childish ones, in their actions, throughout the story. When Albert is left alone, he has to be comforted like a child by his son. When Celie starts to sound like a womanist, she tells Nettie that 'wherever there's a man, there's trouble', reversing an old saying (p. 175). (For comment on Shug's song 'A Good Man is Hard to Find', see **Symbolism**, on **Song**.)

EDUCATION AND LITERACY

The themes of schooling for girls and women's writing help to connect the African and American parts of the story. Nettie teaches Celie in America just as Olivia teaches Tashi in Africa, in secret, because men resent and fear the education of women. The writing of the letters, on both sides of the Atlantic, is a symbol of defiance. Albert will stop it if he can. Even though she is unaware of it, Celie's letters are from the first a record and accusation of neglect and abuse, and Nettie's letters are filled with critical observations on the incompetence and inhumanity of white colonists and of African

men. Writing is seen as a weapon: for many women in the past
letters offered the only available means of writing to express and
share their feelings.

AFRICAN-AMERICAN CULTURE

Nowadays we think first of literature and the other arts, when
considering African-American culture. Alice Walker points out, in
In Search of our Mothers' Gardens and elsewhere, that the creative
energy of her parents' generation and earlier ones, especially among
women, went into homely (but rewarding) activities such as
gardening, cooking, sewing and quilt-making. Then as now, music
had a central place.

The traditional art of quilt-making is satisfying to women. Celie
feels just right for the first time in her life while sewing pieces of
quilt together at the end of letter 27. Some women enjoy it more
than others. Shug's quilting technique is idiosyncratic, using 'long,
crooked stitches' (p. 51). The novel also celebrates the art of
cooking, Shug can cook, as we hear after the move to Memphis:
'collards … chitlins … souse … okra …. blackberry pie … Us eat
and eat' (p. 178). Dancing is another feature of black culture in the
old days. Alice Walker comments elsewhere on the pleasure of
finding a reference to the 'moochie' in Zora Neale Hurston (herself
a noted folklorist), 'a dance that scandalized – and titillated – the
elders in my community when I was a very small child' (*Anything
We Love Can Be Saved*, p. 43). The scandalous and titillating
moochie is danced again in *The Color Purple*: 'Sometime us did the
moochie for an hour' (p. 104) (for more on **quilts**, see **Symbolism**).

> **CONTEXT**
>
> The period
> 1900–40 saw a
> worldwide
> revolution in
> attitudes to
> women's
> education.

The significance of song is obvious throughout. As a theme, it sets
Celie's milieu in its historical place. When Celie mentions 'someone
called Bessie Smith', apparently a friend of Shug's, readers who have
heard recordings of 'the Empress of the Blues' can imagine how
Shug would sing. Celie's casual words, furthermore, are just right:
this is how the famous blues singer would have been mentioned at a
remote jukejoint in the early days. Celie's locality is suddenly
linked with the greater world. (For more on **Song**, see **Symbolism**
and **Historical background**.)

BUSINESS

African-Americans are, after all, Americans, and the novel shows how quickly they prosper in private enterprises once the opportunity exists. Harpo becomes a new man, in Letter 32, when he discovers he is 'smart' at making money. The excitement makes him work long hours at building his jukejoint. Once it is built he makes 'right smart money' (p. 66), and Shug makes money too. Shug works hard at her career and buys the house in Memphis and a second car. New inventions were behind this prosperity in early-twentieth century America: recordings, radio, and motor cars. The car especially gave a sense of excitement and freedom that is conveyed in the novel in motoring scenes. The name of Celie's firm, 'Folkspants, Unlimited' (rather than a merely 'Limited Company'), conveys the spirit of boundless commercial opportunity that swept through the United States, until 'the Great Depression' lowered business confidence after 1929 (not reflected in the novel). The African parts of the narrative remind us of how workpeople can be ill-treated by companies out to make quick profits, as in Letters 58 and 65, for example. But Celie's story stresses that while poverty can almost enslave women, prosperity helps to set them free.

CONTEXT

The Ford Model T (Tin Lizzie) car went into production in America in 1908. Shug probably had one of the first.

VIOLENCE

The fictional presentation of violence is difficult. Unsuccessful attempts to arouse pity through over-insistence on disgusting details tend to numb the reader's response. Walker's purposes in this novel require her to portray many incidents of rape and beating, but these are so tactfully described that the effect is realistic and pitiful.

QUESTION

'The Color Purple depicts many scenes of violence but it is a tender rather than a violent book.' Discuss.

Grotesque aspects of violence appear in Celie's accounts of how she has been abused (p. 97), and the inanity of violence is shown in the descriptions of Sofia's fights with Harpo (p. 36). Sofia's arrest is an extremely emotive scene: a black woman strikes a white official, and the police close in on her. The power of such an incident to arouse emotion does not make it easier to render successfully, without stereotyped effects. Celie's halting description, interrupted by Albert when she breaks down, is simple and strong. More space is given, on the next page, to Celie's caring for Sofia in prison than to her beating and arrest. *The Color Purple* depicts many scenes of violence, but it is a tender rather than a violent book.

RELIGIOUS BELIEF

'Dear God' begins each of the first fifty-one letters and the last, and 'Amen' ends Celie's letters to Nettie, as well as the novel. It is Shug who sets out explicitly the theme of 'Spirit' rather than church religion, which recurs throughout the story. Celie has lost the simple but devout Christian faith which sustained her in early life because God has kept from her the knowledge of her true parentage and divided her from Nettie: she thinks God must have been asleep (p. 151). In her anger she says that 'God … is a man', and that 'if he ever listened to poor colored women the world would be a different place, I can tell you' (p. 164). Shug answers her by insisting that 'God is inside you and inside everybody else' (p. 166).

The mistake, Shug says, is to think of God as an old white man. It is better to think of the trees, and all created things. 'Man corrupt everything,' she declares. You must 'git man off your eyeball' before you can see anything (p. 168). Once the idea of God is freed from false images, however, she or he or it is to be revered and not feared because the old religious taboos, especially on sins of sex, do not apply any more. Celie is eventually converted to this new faith, and her last letter begins 'Dear God. Dear stars, dear trees, dear sky, dear peoples. Dear everything' (p. 242). Even Nettie says that 'God is different to us now … more spirit … and more internal' (p. 218).

Unsympathetic readers may feel that some of the religious talk in the novel is inexact, equating Spirit with matter and love with making love, but even they must admit that it is warm and sincere, and coheres with the belief that all **patriarchal** culture should be overthrown.

 CHECK THE BOOK
Elizabeth Cady Stanton's *The Woman's Bible* (1898) was an early feminist work on religion that has influenced Alice Walker.

NARRATIVE TECHNIQUES

STRUCTURE

The story is firmly constructed, with a desperately dramatic opening, a middle full of conflict and endeavour, and a happy ending. It is a traditional type of story in beginning with the breakup of a family and ending with its reunion. The loving sisters are parted, but restored to each other in spite of all the villain's treachery. Mother and children, torn apart by cruelty, are also reunited, in happier circumstances than could ever have been expected. Virtue is further rewarded, in the cases of Celie and Nettie, by the unlooked-for and timely inheritance of house and property (hitherto wrongly withheld from them).

CHECK THE BOOK

See 'Looking for Jung' in *Anything We Love Can Be Saved* for Walker's views on coincidence. The psychiatrist C. G. Jung (1865-1961) had a theory of 'synchronicity'.

COINCIDENCE

Much of the action depends on coincidence: not only is Nettie befriended by the adoptive parents of Celie's children; Samuel happens (rather improbably given their respective characters and ways of life) to have been an old crony of Alphonso. Furthermore, this means that he knows the secret of the sisters' parentage. The stain of incest is thus removed; Alphonso turns out to be an evil stepfather, as we might have expected. Albert is dramatically changed into a reformed character at the end. The story may remind some readers, especially in its rather leisurely closing stages, of the ways in which Victorian **melodrama** pitted brute force against love and friendship, leaving heroes and heroines well off in every way.

LETTER-WRITING

The use of letters also contributes to the structure. It provides two points of view, and two styles, in the first-person narrators, Celie and Nettie. Letter-writing (and the theft of letters) is part of the story. Each of the sisters writes as an act of faith, keeping up her own spirits in difficult times, and reaching out to the other. Albert, intercepting Nettie's letters, stands in their way, as though forbidding sisterhood.

Use of letters also affects the distribution of incidents in time. The events of a few days are described in one or more of Celie's letters, and then years pass unrecorded. Some of these intervals are noted in the letters; others are not. We sometimes have to calculate the passage of time for ourselves (see **Dating events**). This elliptical method is effective in dealing with the challenge Alice Walker set herself of presenting nearly forty years, from two lives spent mostly apart, in the space of a relatively short novel (about 70,000 words).

THE ENDING

The author's contriving of her story's happy ending is rather noticeable. Corrine dies (repentant, after all her false suspicions) just in time for Nettie to marry Samuel. The sisters inherit property. Just when Celie is ready and able to welcome Nettie, the missionary family returns home. The telegram with false news of Nettie's death ensures that her homecoming will be even more of a happy surprise.

We may accept all this under the convention of the happy ending. But we may be less willing to accept incidents where the author seems to have arranged the evidence to support her themes. Tashi's father is a feeble spokesman for Africa as a man's world, and easily disposed of. Soon after quarrelling with Nettie, he refuses Western medicine and dies of malaria. Many modern African novels in English show how much subtler and tougher a tribal elder might have been, if Alice Walker had allowed. When the bishop who receives Samuel and Nettie in England proves to be foolish and feeble, we are unsurprised because he is obviously akin to Tashi's father in the novel's scheme, which always leaves Nettie in the right.

CHECK THE BOOK

See the novels of the Nigerian, Elechi Amadi.

The danger is that we may feel the author is indulging 'her' characters in ways that undermine her case: we may reflect that missionary work and small businesses, women's roles in African society, and new bearings in theology, are all more difficult and more interesting than Nettie and Celie are permitted to find out. Such thoughts are liable to arise in reading the last series of letters; if that happens, the demands of the happy ending have weakened the novel's power to persuade.

In other ways, however, *The Color Purple* is effective in reworking old conventions for new purposes. Literature constantly renews itself in this way, and Alice Walker has a sure sense of how to tell a story. Not all committed writers are so good-humoured. Her sense of fun adds to many scenes: 'Folkspants, Unlimited' might have become an overworked symbolic ploy in a less deft and exuberant writer.

DATING EVENTS

We are never given the letters' dates. Celie does not record the dates she finds on Nettie's letters. Some letters tell us how many years have passed since the one before; others do not. There is sometimes a vagueness about the passage of time. This is natural: neither sister is keeping a journal. But the way Nettie's letters take us back in time is likely to make us ask ourselves about dates.

A late letter from Nettie offers an approximate date by referring to the approach of a 'big war' (p. 194); this must be late in the 1930s. Since at least two years of the war have passed by the time of Nettie's return to America, the date here must be around 1939. The war has started five letters later; this is presumably to be dated between 1939 and 1941. Nettie gives a useful clue before coming home by saying that it is nearly thirty years since she last saw Celie (p. 217), implying a date around 1912 for their parting in Letter 11. Working back from there, we may suppose that Celie marries Albert in 1911, since they have not been together long when Nettie comes to live with them, and her need to escape from Alphonso is urgent once Celie's protection is removed. Celie reports the meeting with Corrine where Olivia is said to be six years old in her tenth letter (pp. 14–16); so the first letter must belong to the period 1904–5. Celie must have been born about 1890.

CHECK THE FILM
Olivia is a baby in this scene in the film, which uses a different time-scheme.

We can try to work forward from the date of Celie's marriage. Harpo is then twelve (p. 13). He is seventeen when he first talks about Sofia; this must be about 1916 (p. 22). So far he has only managed to wink at Sofia in church; when they marry, her first baby is 'a big ole nursing boy', so we must allow at least another year: Harpo brings Sofia and the baby home in 1917 or 1918 (p. 32). The next letter says that Harpo and Sofia have been married three years, bringing us to about 1920; it is at least 1921 when she leaves him because they now have five children. This is about the time of Shug Avery's arrival, sick, to stay with Albert and Celie. Since Shug stays on only to persuade Albert to stop beating Celie, after her recovery, Sofia's return ought not to be more than two years later; Shug is still singing at Harpo's place then. 1924 must be the approximate date for the events of the letters covering Sofia's imprisonment (pp.

75–86). Celie says that Sofia was in prison for three years before starting to work as a maid for Miss Millie (p. 87). We are now in 1927. Two more years of Sofia's sentence have passed in the next letter when she sees her children (p. 89), making it 1929.

Shug's return at Christmas in the next letter is difficult to date. It must be some years later, although no mention is made of the passage of time. It is during this visit that Celie and Shug find the letters from Nettie. The first letter from Nettie that Celie reads says that the family are already planning to return to America. We must be well into the 1930s. That is confirmed by the fact that Sofia has been released from prison after eleven and a half years of her sentence, as we know from the letter where Celie is still angry with Albert about his suppression of the correspondence (p. 169). This is 1935 or 1936.

Nettie's encounter with Sofia (pp. 110–12) is impossible to date, if we accept this scheme. Sofia is working as Miss Millie's maid, which means a date on or after 1927. Nettie is about to leave for Africa, and it is this meeting that persuades her to go. But Olivia and Adam would be adults by this time, and they are plainly young children when first in Africa. Her earliest letters (pp. 107–12) show that Nettie leaves for Africa soon after her parting from Celie, which is about 1912. Her first letter (p. 107) is written just after Nettie's flight, and the next says that it is too soon to hope for a reply. By the next, Nettie is 'almost crazy' at having had no reply. But it is clear that weeks, or just possibly months, have passed, not years. Nettie's fourth letter (p. 110) tells us in a headnote from Celie (unique in referring to a date) that it is dated two months after the last, and Nettie is now writing from Africa.

There are other odd features of the time-scheme. Adam and Tashi are in their thirties when they marry, about 1941, yet they behave as though at an earlier stage of life. Events among the Olinka do not seem to fit such a long span of years as the novel requires. But stories and plays often use a time-scheme that would not work in the actual world; it is best to keep the calendar roughly in mind, but not to worry about it pedantically.

CONTEXT

Historical events are mostly in the distant background. We hear only one reference, for example, to the First World War (p. 194).

 QUESTION

'The story runs from the early years of the twentieth century up to the 1940s. Apart from that, we are not meant to think in terms of dates.' Discuss.

LANGUAGE AND STYLE

SOUTHERN DIALECT

Celie's letters are marked by dialect features. Conjugation, especially of 'be' and 'have', is jumbled. Final 's' is often irregular ('two mens', 'she say'). Archaisms still common in many dialects occur, such as the double negative, and the form 'ain't' ('She ain't never no good!'). The pronoun system is non-standard: 'us' serves for 'we' as well as 'us'; 'they' serves for 'they' and 'their'. Phonetic spellings convey the sound of speech: 'ast' for 'asked' and 'ask'. With relatively few deviations of this kind from standard grammar, Walker creates a remarkably expressive style. The text always remains easy reading, however, by contrast, say, to the rich but difficult prose in novels of the American South by William Faulkner (1897–1962). Southern American vocabulary and idioms give us the feel of everyday life. Thinking of horse-thieves or 'hants' makes folks nervous when opening the door at night (p. 36). If hair is 'nappy' (p. 49), it can be 'cornrowed' (p. 51). There may be 'grits' (p. 46) or 'clabber' (p. 55) for breakfast or 'chitlins' (p. 63) and 'souse' (p. 178) for dinner. In a community where white people are few and uninteresting, skins are not black or white but black, like Shug's, or yellow like Squeak's, or bright like Sofia's. Shoes or a song or talk may be sassy (saucy). If a preacher has got his mouth on somebody (p. 40) it may be because she has the nasty woman's disease (p. 49). Other diseases are hard to be sure about, including mysterious 'two berkulosis' (p. 40). Down at the jukejoint, they dance the 'moochie' and some smoke 'reefer'.

The novel shows its author's knowledge of the **oral culture** of the old South, on which all speakers can draw. When Celie tells Albert how she has coaxed the convalescent Shug into eating some breakfast, and says that nobody living can resist the smell of home-cured ham, she adds, 'If they dead they got a chance. Maybe' (p. 47), and even Albert laughs. He and Celie have heard the joke, in the same words, many times; and so has Alice Walker.

INNOCENT NARRATORS

The Color Purple can be seen as part of a long tradition of American fiction, going back to *Huckleberry Finn* (1884) by Mark Twain

CHECK THE BOOK

See the stories in *Go Down Moses* (1942) for a first taste of Faulkner.

(pseudonym of Samuel Langhorne Clemens, 1835–1910). In novels of this kind a young or innocent narrator tells the story in dialect and uneducated English and with a much less mature understanding than the novel expects of the reader. *The Catcher in the Rye* (1951) by J. D. Salinger (b.1919) is another such work. The style of these young narrators has the attractions of lively speech. Like Twain's Huck Finn and Salinger's Holden Caulfield, the young Celie writes the early letters in a style close to the way she speaks, and although her later writing matures, it does not lose its frank appeal.

CHECK THE FILM
There are several screen versions of *Huckleberry Finn*, the classic American tale of escape from slavery.

CELIE'S STYLE

The earliest letters establish her in our sympathy. They often have a breathless immediacy:

> Dear God,
> He act like he can't stand me no more. Say I'm evil an always up to no good. He took my other little baby, a boy this time. But I don't think he kilt it.   (p. 5)

Declining to name 'him' seems natural: this is how children talk. This style adds to the concentrated impact of the opening letters, and anyway, God knows who she is talking about.

Some of the best writing in the novel comes in Celie's curt notes on the horrific world she grows up in: 'His wife died. She was kilt by her boyfriend coming home from church' (p. 6). This is how she introduces the murder of Harpo's mother, an episode more fully described in later letters. The childish brevity, which makes the killing appear more of an everyday, unremarkable incident than it later turns out to have been, sets the right tone of gratuitous violence for Celie's early vision of the world. Celie's later letters grow in fluency, in telling use of detail and in grasp of motive, but she remains an uncomplicated, straightforward narrator. Comparison of the first letter and the one where Celie tells Shug how Alphonso used to abuse her (pp. 96–7) shows how her style develops. Our impression of crudity on first reading the third paragraph of Letter 1 is dispelled as soon as we sense the limits of the girl's vocabulary and understanding. The blunt description conveys exactly the emotion the author wants. The later letter puts the same incident into an adult context. In bed with Shug, Celie relives the misery in detail, recalling how the dripping blood 'mess up' (p. 96) her stocking. There is an intimacy and an air of integrity about Celie's odd grammar in such passages: she remembers 'how much I was surprise' by the rape, and here her dialect helps to make her real in our imagination.

CONTEXT

Such images are typical of blues lyrics.

Celie is a lively and witty writer. Questions run through her mind 'like snakes' (p. 26). When Shug first appears, seriously ill but flamboyant as usual, Celie says, 'She look like she ain't long for this world but dressed well for the next' (p. 42); Shug is 'skinny as a bean, and her face full of eyes' (p. 51). Good touches such as these enliven Celie's letters throughout.

Celie's letters are mostly in short paragraphs full of fast-moving action and lots of dialogue. Nettie's letters are in longer paragraphs of standard English, tending to relate in a formal manner states of affairs in her own family and among the Olinka people.

CHECK THE BOOK

See *Alice Walker Banned* by Patricia Holt (1996).

OFFENSIVE LANGUAGE

Attempts have occasionally been made to remove the novel from school syllabuses in the United States. (Older classics such as *Huckleberry Finn* have been targeted in the same way.) One charge that is sometimes made against *The Color Purple* is that it contains 'bad language'. Alice Walker has attempted to answer this objection, in a paper called 'Coming in from the Cold', which she read at conferences in America two years after the novel's publication, when it had already become a text set for study in schools. This paper gives a particular example of a parent in California who appealed to her local school board against the use of *The Color Purple* as a set book on the grounds (among others) that it was 'too sexually explicit'.

Walker's essay begins by acknowledging that some of the novel's language can cause offence. She admits that her own mother was shocked by language in the opening pages, and goes on to say that she tried to modify the tone of the first letter where Celie speaks of 'pussy', 'titties' and the man's 'thing': 'I remember actually trying to censor this passage in Celie's voice as I wrote it. Even I found it almost impossible to let her say what had happened to her as *she perceived it, without euphemising a little'* (*Living by the Word*, p. 57). She then decided that it was wrong to deny Celie her own voice from a squeamish reluctance – even if natural enough – to recognise that such sexual abuse really does happen. She points out that Celie would know no other words than the ones used. The essay concludes by asserting that the alternative of using 'pretty, distancing' language that might have avoided or minimised offence would have been a betrayal of Celie, since the use of her own language is an essential part of her integrity.

For more on language and style, including style in Nettie's letters, see **Text 2, Extended commentaries.**

QUESTION

How does use of language reveal character, and especially the character of Celie, in *The Color Purple*?

SYMBOLISM

PURPLE

The title points to the imaginative design. Purple is the colour of a bruise. When Sofia has been beaten by the police she is the colour of 'an eggplant' (p. 77). Purple is also the colour of the robes of royalty and nobility, of Roman emperors and English lords. This is why Celie thinks it the colour Shug Avery would choose to wear: 'She like a queen to me, so I say to [Albert's sister] Kate, Somethin purple, maybe little red in it too' (p. 20). Red goes with purple, in stately robes and imperial pomp. There is no purple in the store, and even red would be too expensive for Albert; but Celie later makes pants of purple, red, and every other bright colour. But it is the contrast between bruised and battered victims and the queenly, triumphant figures women can become when they are free that gives *The Color Purple* its basic structure. Celie makes pants for Sofia with one leg red and the other one purple and then dreams of her wearing them and 'jumping over the moon' (p. 184). Celie has her room painted purple and red (p. 240). The colour of bruises has become the noblest of colours by the end of the novel.

CONTEXT

An English poet has also celebrated purple: 'When I am an old woman I shall wear purple/With a red hat that doesn't go' (Jenny Joseph, 'Warning', 1974).

Shug gives a new significance to the colour purple when she explains her religious belief to Celie, saying that 'it pisses God off if you walk by the color purple in a field somewhere and don't notice it' (p. 167). The very existence of purple is wonderful, and therefore a symbol of the wonder of existence which is the core of the new faith Shug and Celie share.

FOLKSPANTS, UNLIMITED

Pants, or trousers, are another symbol of women's emancipation. When Shug first sings in the jukejoint, her skin-tight red dress shocks and excites the audience (and helps to get her criticised from the pulpit at church). The wearing of pants (slacks or casual trousers), still very unusual at this date as a garment for women, is also daring. Celie is hesitant when Shug first talks about pants, even though she has envied the red dress and regretted that she has only dull 'churchgoing' clothes in her wardrobe (p. 64). Once she has started to make and wear pants, however, after the move to Memphis, Celie fills the house with them, in all the colours of the rainbow. She and Shug both take delight in bright colours. They go for a drive, for example, wearing 'our new blue flower pants that match' (p. 152). Wearing slacks offers comfort and ease after the constrictions of nineteenth-century costume. Their design makes them cheerful and erotic. Pants also signify a new, unsubmissive attitude towards men, who formerly were the only ones to wear the trousers.

Making pants changes from a hobby to a business when Celie launches 'Folkspants, Unlimited', and so symbolises emancipation in a new way: nowadays women can make big money. For Celie, however, pants are more poetic than commercial, clothes in which to jump over the moon.

CHECK THE NET

For all about quilts and quilting, see **http://ttsw.com/ MainQuiltingPage .html**.

QUILTS

Making quilts is associated with laughter and relaxation, as when Sofia and Celie are united in sewing quilts at the end of Letter 21. It could be said that pants and pants-making and Celie's firm 'Folkspants, Unlimited' create a symbol of freedom in the modern world, while quilts and quilt making, a traditional occupation allowing women to work together and share pieces of cloth among themselves, symbolise women's solidarity, past and present.

THE MAILBOX

There is one short sentence in Letter 28, which simply mentions that Shug and Albert walk to the mailbox. On a first reading of the novel we may hardly notice this narrative detail, but it is sure to catch our attention once we know the whole story.

Celie and Nettie both write letters that seem to be desperate measures. Celie writes hers to God. Nettie posts her letters from Africa with little hope of Celie's receiving them. On the voyage out she scatters fragments of a letter on the sea, almost in despair at ever making contact with her sister again. The mailbox makes it easy for Albert to intercept Nettie's incoming letters, but it always holds the promise of a day when one may get through to Celie at last, and its day does come.

Letters 49-51 make a dramatic turning-point in the story. Letter 49 begins with Celie clutching a letter, from Nettie! Then we learn how Shug noticed foreign stamps on letters that Albert was pocketing. Then comes the revelation of a trunk full of old letters hidden away, like a second mailbox from which a new dimension of the story opens up.

The mailbox is a conspicuous object in Spielberg's film *The Color Purple*, and appropriately so because it is such a powerful symbol. It stands for the promise and then the realisation of contact between the sisters. It also stands for the modern world of travel and communication, in contrast to Albert's little realm (see **Background, on Spielberg's film**).

SONG

Shug sings 'A Good Man is Hard to Find' at Harpo's jukejoint, a famous song sung in the 1920s by Bessie Smith, one of the real blues singers mentioned in the book. It sometimes seems that the whole novel is an illustration of the theme of that song. Black American songs evolved from the 'field hollers' and other singing of slaves in the plantations. In the blues which swept America in the 1920s, black men and women sang of lives of poverty and hardship with courage and humour and in a very distinctive style. In *The Color*

CHECK THE NET

For more about the blues, see **www. blues.org/history/**

Purple it is the women who sing – of their wrongs, as when Squeak sings 'They calls me yellow' (p. 85), or when the song Shug dedicates to 'Miss Celie' is about 'some man doing her wrong' (p. 65).

The huge success of the blues and of jazz made rapid fortunes for star performers, as it makes Shug's fortune too. The novel shows what a symbol of courage and hope that triumph was. It is ironic that black Americans continued to suffer neglect and contempt even when their music was the height of fashion. But the singing of the great Queen Honeybees symbolises their people's extraordinary spirit of resolve (see **Themes**, on **African-American culture**, and **Historical background**).

RAZOR

Slave narratives show that a man's razor was often used to compel a woman slave to submit. Albert does not know the danger he is in when Celie stands behind him holding his razor, after she has learnt of how he has hidden Nettie's letters. Shug disarms her and later persuades her to choose the needle to sew pants rather than the razor as an instrument of revenge, as Celie says herself (p. 125). As for Shug, she has a razor in her smile: 'she smile,' says Celie, 'like a razor opening' (p. 51). The film uses the razor as a symbol of deadly intent even more conspicuously than the novel and brings out a parallel with ritual cutting in Africa (see **Background**, on **Spielberg's film**).

'DEAR TREES'

CONTEXT

Alice Walker founded Wild Trees Press, a publishing company, in 1985.

Roofleaf is symbolic of traditional African values and way of life (see **Text 2** of **Extended commentaries**). Roofleaf in Africa is connected with Shug's and Celie's celebration of trees as symbols of nature and the wonder of nature. 'Dear God. Dear stars, dear trees' Celie prays at the start of the last letter (p. 242).

CRITICAL HISTORY

The Color Purple quickly divided intellectual opinion among African-Americans. Many men attacked the book and the film on political grounds, arguing that the stress on violence and cruelty in the portrayal of the central black male characters threatened the unity of the African-American community and its struggle for civil rights. In *The Same River Twice* Alice Walker reprints some of the attacks (she was denounced as 'a liar, a whore, a traitor'), including an article in the *Carolina Peacemaker* in 1986 which endorsed *Time*'s summary, 'Walker's message: "Sisterhood is beautiful and Men stink"' (p. 224). In mounting her defence, Walker became perhaps the novel's most prolific and interesting interpreter. *The Same River Twice* reprints sympathetic reviews, dozens of enthusiastic letters from readers, offers views on various aspects of the novel, and gives a detailed account of Walker's involvement in the making of the film (including her screenplay, rejected by Spielberg).

One recurring theme in this volume is Walker's disappointment at Spielberg's having all but excluded the lesbian relationship, and another is that Albert is portrayed 'unforgivingly', that is, as a wholly unsympathetic character. The Albert of the novel, she insists, is a complex and many-layered creation, written from love of the spirit of black men (a spirit alive in herself) as well as from hatred of male abuse of women.

Among black women, critics have not always been well disposed. A notable adverse critic is bell hooks, whose essay of 1990 (see **Further reading**) attacks the novel for failing to present its lesbian theme in an adequate political framework. Celie's relationship with Shug is seen as a purely personal affair, which provokes none of the hostility that homosexuality often arouses in modern society. Furthermore, Shug and Celie succeed in business by accepting the heterosexual and capitalist society about them. It could be said that they surrender to 'the American Dream'. hooks' is a thoughtful article written from a more radical feminist position than Alice Walker's.

 QUESTION

Some critics compare Alice Walker's novels to the quilts her characters make, patching pieces together. Do you think *The Color Purple* is like this, or has it a more complex structure?

Many of the most interesting interpretations in recent years have come from feminists. One area of disagreement concerns the concept of **realism**. A particularly good critical essay is Andrea Stuart's '*The Color Purple*: In Defence of Happy Endings' in *The Female Gaze* (1988). Stuart defends the novel against charges that the plot is too dependent on coincidences and that the concept of spirit is inadequate ('wishy-washy') by arguing that it should be read not as 'a realist novel in the ordinary sense' but rather as a folk tale or a fable in the tradition of the Uncle Remus stories (see **The text** on Letter 64 and **Background,** on **Commitments** 'which advocate tolerance, patience, perseverance and cunning for the underdog's survival' (p. 65).

Others disagree. bell hooks insists that Walker has committed herself to the realist tradition going back to the early **slave narratives** and **black** protest writing in the nineteenth century, which aimed to tell the truth about slavery and its aftermath. Conditions among black women in early-twentieth-century America, *The Color Purple* declares, really were as the novel portrays them, with no admixture of fantasy or fable-making or Uncle Remus. hooks acknowledges this realist commitment but objects that it is betrayed by the happy ending, which buries the public issues in the characters' private emotions. What of Sofia, the revolutionary, for whom there is no happy ending?

Renée C. Hoogland supports bell hooks in reading the novel 'in the tradition of social realism'. Noting that violet and lavender were emblematic of lesbianism in antiquity, Hoogland argues that Walker fails to be realistic enough because she does not understand the implications of her lesbian theme. Shug and Celie are content to enjoy their relationship in private, without challenging the **patriarchal** and heterosexual society about them.

Barbara Christian's *Black Feminist Criticism: Perspectives on Black Women Writers* discusses *The Color Purple* in the context of contemporary African-American fiction. Like Walker herself, Barbara Christian emphasises that a novelist must treat history as a human activity. A novel is not written about slavery or about racism, but about people, presented as characters, whose lives are injured by slavery or racism.

CHECK THE NET

For more information, search for 'slave narratives'.

Another strength of Barbara Christian's work is her good ear for verse and prose. She brings out the point that however grim the stories and themes of Alice Walker's novels, they attract attention by 'the personal grace that distinguishes her voice' (p. 82). Professor Christian writes attractively herself.

CHECK THE BOOK
Walker's poems were collected as *Her Blue Body Everything We Know: Earthling Poems 1965–1990 Complete.*

The central place the novel has won in women's studies can be seen from a collection called *Women's Studies and Culture: A Feminist Introduction* (1995), where Hoogland's article appears. This volume includes essays on literary theory, history, film studies, art history, musicology, lesbian studies and semiotics, all of which discuss *The Color Purple*.

Some of these essays point out that not all Alice Walker's basic assumptions are very different from old patriarchal ones, such as belief in human nature, and in the transforming power of love. Nor is she very radical in her critical conceptions. She believes in fictional characters with their own odd kind of reality, and in authors with intentions that readers can get right or wrong. Where conventional readers have been shocked by the novel, several recent critics have seen Walker as a traditional humanist. Liesbeth Brouwer, writing in *Women's Studies and Culture*, finds *The Color Purple* 'the perfect emancipation novel', but also 'a novel which inscribes women in a familiar tale: it reproduces the modernist (here meaning traditional) and liberal democratic ideology which defines a task for women and men alike, that is, to strive for a fulfilled life' (p. 158).

BACKGROUND

ALICE WALKER

SHORT BIOGRAPHY

CHECK THE BOOK
For more on Walker's life, see her essays (including 'Father') in *Living by the Word*.

Alice Malsenior Walker was born in 1944 in Eatonton, Georgia, in the Deep South of the United States, the youngest child of a sharecropper (a tenant farmer who supplies a share of his crop to the landlord in place of rent). An accident blinded her in one eye when she was eight. She has said that she became more shy, thoughtful and studious as a result, and began to write stories.

She went to Spelman College (for black women) in Atlanta, Georgia, in 1961, transferring to Sarah Lawrence College, New York, in 1963. Here she read widely in many literatures, and took her degree in 1965. She won a writing scholarship for the following year, and in the next two decades held a series of fellowships, awards and teaching appointments, including posts at Wellesley College and Yale University. She married Melvyn R. Levanthal, a Civil Rights lawyer, in 1967; their daughter Rebecca was born in 1969; they were divorced in 1976.

CHECK THE NET
For the Civil Rights Movement, see http://search.eb.com/blackhistory/micro/129/80.html.

A speech by Martin Luther King persuaded her to return to the South. She and her husband lived in the state of Mississippi from 1967 to 1974, illegally married, as she emphasizes, because Levanthal was legally white. There they were involved in the Civil Rights Movement, which fought to end segregation and to guarantee voting rights for black Americans.

The making of the film *The Color Purple* (1985), adapted from her third novel, changed her life in ways she has described in *The Same River Twice*. She worked closely with Steven Spielberg and his team. After the film's appearance she was involved in fierce controversy within the black community in the United States (see **Reading** *The Color Purple*, and **Critical history**). In 1985 she founded, with Robert Allen, a publishing company, Wild Trees Press.

Since then she has combined the life of a prolific author with work on behalf of individuals (including Winnie Mandela and Salman Rushdie) and public causes, especially the ending of apartheid in South Africa and the campaign against female genital mutilation. In spite of ill health, she has travelled and addressed audiences all over the world.

It is for *The Color Purple* that Alice Walker is best known, the novel's readership greatly enlarged after the success of the film. It has become a feminist classic (and all but a sacred text), and won the admiration of countless readers, not only feminists, by the warmth and sharpness with which its author wrote about life.

CHECK THE BOOK

On female genital mutilation and the film *Warrior Marks,* see Walker's essay 'Heaven Belongs to You', in *Anything We Love Can Be Saved.*

OTHER WORKS BY ALICE WALKER

Walker was a prolific and successful writer from an early age. Her essay 'The Civil Rights Movement: What Good Was It?' won a prize offered by the *American Scholar* in 1967. Her first short story, 'To Hell With Dying', was also published in 1967. *Once: Poems* (1968) was followed by several other collections of her verse. Her first novel, *The Third Life of Grange Copeland*, appeared in 1970. Set in the Deep South, this book follows the family history of the Copelands through three generations, in violent times, showing how racism injured the lives of black people. Grange Copeland reacts to his sense of humiliation by acts of violence against women. Her second novel *Meridian* (1976) also prefigures *The Color Purple*. The heroine is a modern woman, involved in the Civil Rights Movement, but also passionately concerned with the past traditions and present predicament of black women. *In Love and Trouble: Stories of Black Women* (1973) and *You Can't Keep A Good Woman Down* (1981) are collections of her short stories. *The Way Forward is with a Broken Heart* (2000) is a collection of stories that 'merge fiction and fact'. Walker's essays have been collected in three books: *In Search of Our Mothers' Gardens: Womanist Prose* (1983); *Living by the Word: Selected Writings 1973-87* (1981); and *Anything We Love Can Be Saved: A Writer's Activism* (1997). Her critical studies include *Langston Hughes: American Poet* (1974).

CONTEXT

Like *The Color Purple, Meridian* has a strong and telling title, with a cluster of meanings (including 'South' and 'high point') set out on its first page.

Her commitment to feminism, or in her preferred term, womanism, inspired *The Color Purple* (1982) and its successors, *The Temple of My Familiar* (1989) and *Possessing the Secret of Joy* (1992), novels which continue the story of Celie's people in more recent times. *By the Light of My Father's Smile* (1998) also develops themes present in *The Color Purple*, especially 'the sexual healing of the soul' (in the words of its subtitle). *Possessing the Secret of Joy* develops a concern which appears in some of Nettie's later letters in *The Color Purple*, female genital mutilation (female circumcision). Alice Walker collaborated with Pratibha Parmar to make a film, *Warrior Marks*, and to write a book (1993) of the same title, protesting against this practice.

COMMITMENTS

Alice Walker's life and writing are connected in various ways, especially in her firm commitments to feminism and to the long campaign against racism. Her essays and memoirs often cast light on this background to her fiction by drawing on her life and opinions to illustrate and support her strongly held allegiances.

The first of these is to a sisterhood of heroines often mentioned in her essays (and sometimes recipients of dedications to novels), and warmly cherished. Some come from the age of slavery, notably Harriet Tubman (1820-1913), famous for her success in rescuing slaves from the southern states, using the 'Underground Railway' of secret routes and safe houses, by means of which Tubman herself had escaped from slavery in Maryland in 1849. Others are women of the jazz age, including Bessie Smith, one of whose songs Shug sings in the novel (see above p. 91) and Mamie Smith (1883-1946), whose song 'You Can't Keep a Good Man Down' is echoed in the title of Walker's essay collection, *You Can't Keep a Good Woman Down*. Other heroines are writers, notably Zora Neale Hurston (see **Literary background**).

CHECK THE NET
For more about Harriet Tubman, see **www.nyhistory. com/harriet tubman**.

The ex-slave Sojourner Truth is the heroine of Alice Walker's who is most relevant to *The Color Purple*. Walker tells us how inspiring she finds the famous occasion when this champion of women's rights and powerful public speaker quelled an unruly audience by baring her breasts and thundering 'Ain't I a Woman?' In her essay, 'A Name is Sometimes an ancestor saying Hi, I'm With You', Walker claims Sojourner Truth as 'a spiritual ancestor', and notices a link between their names. 'Sojourner ("Walker" – in the sense of traveller, journeyer, wanderer) Truth (which "Alice" means in Old

Greek) is also my name. How happy I was when I realised this... I get a power from this name that [we] share... That irrepressible great heart rises in my chest...' (*Living by the Word*, pp. 97-8). There are passages in *The Color Purple* which recall this great heart, especially in the scene in which Celie makes her resounding declaration of independence to Albert, in Letter 75: 'I'm here' (See **Extended commentaries, Text 3**). Celie repeatedly asserts in this scene that her words 'ain't just coming from me' (p. 176). Wherever they come from, they recall the defiant spirit of Sojourner Truth.

**CHECK
THE BOOK**
*Narrative of
Sojourner Truth* was
published in 1850
(reissued 1997).

Opposition to racism in Alice Walker is connected with the affirmation of African-American culture. The culture the slaves brought from Africa survived in stories as well as in songs, and such stories are the subject of her essay 'The Dummy in the Window' (collected in *Living by the Word*). Here she discusses the relevance of folklore to her fiction and focuses on the animal fables of 'Uncle Remus'. These are mentioned in *The Color Purple* when Olivia tells one of the stories to Tashi and is surprised to find that the Olinka people know the tales in their original form (p.140). Walker's essay describes how Alice as a child heard the same stories from her parents before she found out about Joel Chandler Harris' versions in the *Uncle Remus* books. This supports critics such as Andrea Stuart (See **Critical history**) who maintain that *The Color Purple* was influenced by traditional animal fables. It comes as a shock, therefore, when Walker's essay proceeds to attack Harris as a white man who appropriated African folklore and removed the stories from their place in African-American culture. Walker's repudiation of J.C. Harris is all the more startling because they share a hometown in Eatonton, Georgia. It is a stern reminder of the bitter divisiveness of southern American history and of Alice Walker's uncompromising commitment to the cause of her own people.

HISTORICAL BACKGROUND

The background is the history of black people, especially women, in the southern United States in the period between the later nineteenth century and the Second World War, and in Africa during the same (colonial) period.

Alice Walker has argued that the history of black women in modern America should be seen in three stages: the first, ending in the 1930s, and the second, ending in the 1950s, can be seen in *The Color Purple*; the third period corresponds to Walker's adult lifetime. (See the interviews reported by M.H. Washington, *Black American Literature Forum*, vol. 11, 1977, pp. 22–4.)

She calls the first period a time of 'Suspended' life for women, because they were lost in a period that offered no hope of progress. It began with the aftermath of the Civil War. When the Union of the Northern states, under President Abraham Lincoln (1809–65), defeated the Confederacy of Southern states in 1865, slavery was abolished throughout the United States by the 13th Amendment to the Constitution, ratified in December 1865. The 14th Amendment of the following year granted citizenship and equal civil rights to the four million ex-slaves. The 15th Amendment reinforced the right of all Americans to vote, in 1870. Northerners felt satisfied with these measures, and did not closely concern themselves with what actually took place in the South. Although black people were free, they were still poor, and easy targets for injustice. Although black men could legally own property and exercise power, as we see in *The Color Purple*, their right to hold property was in effect precarious; they had little hope of redress when it was taken from them. The father of Celie and Nettie was lynched because his business had become a threat to his white rivals. The condition of women was little changed. They laboured in the fields as before, and were, in a phrase of the black woman novelist Zora Neale Hurston that Walker often quotes, 'the mules of the world', laden with every sort of social burden. The reader is shown how these women toiled, insulted and abused by men, black and white. In *The Third Life of Grange Copeland* (1970) and in *The Color Purple* (1982), Alice Walker has been particularly concerned to emphasise the stifling of creative talent in the women of this unhappy era.

The women of Alice Walker's second historical phase are said to have been 'assimilated', during the 1940s and 1950s, 'into the mainstream of American life'. This brought a danger of separation from their ethnic background. In the closing stages of *The Color Purple*, the principal female characters, Celie, Shug, Sofia and Mary

CONTEXT

The economy and social order of the former slave-states had been shattered by the Civil War.

Agnes, are free from the 'suspended' condition of drudgery in which they were all born at the end of the nineteenth century, and are prospering as professional singers and businesswomen in the early 1940s. The positive side of their achievement is highlighted in this novel, but we see signs of difficulty in race relations in Sofia's troubled dealings with the white woman Eleanor Jane.

Walker's third phase, a time of 'emergent' women, began with the Civil Rights Movement of the 1960s, although thoroughly liberated women belonging to earlier periods appear in her novels; we might consider Shug Avery in *The Color Purple* to be one of them. The novelist herself certainly corresponds to her own definition of a woman of this latest age, 'called to life' by the struggles of the 1960s to fight segregation on buses and in restaurants and to achieve full equality for black citizens. The essays of *In Search of Our Mothers' Gardens* include a tribute to Dr Martin Luther King (1929–68), the orator and moral leader of the Movement. Walker emphasises in many essays that the Movement changed human attitudes in the American South. The outlook of her mother, who brought up eight children of her own and lots more besides, and believed that black people were inferior to white, belongs to the 'Suspended' era of the past (*In Search of Our Mothers' Gardens*, p. 123).

The Women's Movement is the other modern movement that has deeply influenced Alice Walker, and it has become her foremost commitment. Her loyalties were divided when she was obliged to criticise sexism among fellow Civil Rights activists. Her second novel, *Meridian* (1976), depicts a highly principled young woman, working in the Civil Rights Movement, who adopts a peaceful but feminist programme in place of the masculine goal of violent revolution. By the time she wrote *The Color Purple*, Walker had decided that she must risk male hostility by an unswerving commitment to the plight of black women abused by men of their own race.

 CHECK THE NET
Search for 'Malcolm X' to learn more about violent goals in the Civil Rights Movement.

The African setting of the novel is less precisely located than the scenes in Georgia and Tennessee. The heroine's sister Nettie is a missionary in West Africa between about 1914 and about 1941. Most of the continent was then under colonial rule. We hear of the

Belgian Congo and of Senegal, where the boat taking Nettie out from England makes a stop at the then French-colonial capital, Dakar. Her next stop is in Liberia, which was an independent state created in the nineteenth century as a refuge for black immigrants returning to Africa from the United States. Rubber planting in the territory of the Olinka people, among whom Nettie works in the novel, suggests a setting in Liberia, where rubber was extensively introduced in the 1920s. But Nettie has sailed on from Liberia and seems, from the stamps on her letters and other indications, to be in a British colony. The ruthless character of the road-building and rubber-planting which destroy the homes, fields and way of life of the Olinka are clearly intended to show the treatment of African peoples under colonialism throughout the continent, and not merely one particular case of bad administration.

Religious practice and beliefs are another feature of the background. Protestant Christianity was quickly absorbed into the culture brought to America from Africa during the era of slavery (from the seventeenth to the nineteenth century). Fostered by songs, music and passionate preaching, the Christian faith remained strong among black people after Emancipation. The appeal of 'the black church' to its women can be seen in *The Third Life of Grange Copeland* (1970) and in *Meridian* (1976). It has been suggested that Southern Baptist sermons may have influenced Walker's choice of the form of letters to God for her third novel, since it was common for preachers to tell of their talks with the Lord, and Celie would have heard them.

CHECK THE BOOK
On the blues and literature, see Houston A. Baker, Jr, *Blues, Ideology and Afro-American Literature* (1984).

Most of the novel is set in the golden age of jazz and blues singing. 'Duke' Ellington (1899–1974) and Bessie Smith (1894–1937) are among the great artists and entertainers mentioned. Other women singers of the blues whose rapid careers in the 1920s resemble Shug Avery's in the novel include Ma Rainey, Mother of the Blues (1886–1939) and Mamie Smith (1883–1946). Recordings (so-called 'race records') and radio, as well as fashionable clubs in New York, spread around the world a style of singing and dancing which had originated in the work songs of slaves (see **Themes**, on **African-American culture**). The great jazz and blues singers of this time managed to reflect ordinary life and a humorous, brave, 'sassy' attitude to life in their songs. Furthermore, the independent, flamboyant lives of these women were in stark contrast to those of women like Celie. In the character of Shug Avery, we see a reflection of their flair and creative spirit.

 QUESTION

Discuss *The Color Purple* as an historical novel.

LITERARY BACKGROUND

Alice Walker is among the best known and most admired of the many black women novelists from the South of the United States whose work has been published during the last twenty years, a group that includes Toni Morrison (see **Further reading**). Earlier writers who influenced this new school of novelists, and Alice Walker in particular, are Zora Neale Hurston, whose novel *Their Eyes Were Watching God* (Harper Collins, 1995) first appeared in 1937, and Margaret Walker (b.1915), author of the epic novel of black American life, *Jubilee* (Bantam, 1995, originally published 1966). Walker calls Zora Neale Hurston (whom she has written about and edited) her 'literary progenitor'. She admires Hurston's 'complete, undiminished sense of self'. She has aimed to imitate Hurston's ability 'to let her characters be themselves, funny talk and all', and she admires the way that Hurston was 'incapable of being embarrassed by anything black people did, and so was able to write about everything' (*In Search of Our Mothers' Gardens*, p. 259). A passage in the opening pages of *Their Eyes Were Watching God*, where Janie learns about life from her grandmother (Nanny), has deeply impressed Alice Walker. Nanny tells Janie that the white man is the ruler of the world, and therefore throws down his burden and hands it to the black man.

 CHECK THE NET

For Zora Neale Hurston, see **http://www-hsc. usc.edu/ ~gallaher/ hurston/hurston. html**.

> 'He pick it up because he have to but he don't tote [carry] it. He hand it to his womanfolks. De nigger woman is de mule uh de world ...'

Grandmother goes on to say that she prays life will be different for Janie. So it is, and so life becomes for Celie and her people, but Walker intends that 'the mules of the world' will never be forgotten.

Among other black American writers who have influenced her work, she mentions with special praise Jean Toomer (1894–1967),

CHECK THE NET
Search for 'Harlem Renaissance' to learn more about Hurston, Toomer, and their world.

poet, playwright and fiction-writer, whose novel *Cane* (Norton, 1988, originally published 1923) was a major work of the movement called the Harlem Renaissance; and the poet, songwriter, playwright, novelist and musician Langston Hughes (1902–67), whom Toomer influenced, and about whom Walker has written a book. She notes of Toomer that 'he has a very feminine sensibility', adding 'unlike most black male writers' (*In Search of Our Mothers' Gardens*, p. 259).

Alice Walker has acknowledged the influence of many writers in other traditions. Among white women writers she admires are the Brontë sisters, Anne (1820–49), Charlotte (1816–55) and Emily (1818–48); Doris Lessing (b.1919), whose work draws on her upbringing in Zimbabwe (then Southern Rhodesia), and whose novel *The Golden Notebook* (Paladin 1989, originally published 1962) treats themes from feminist points of view; and Simone de Beauvoir (1908–86), the French novelist and essayist, author of a key feminist work, translated as *The Second Sex* (translated by H.M. Parshley, Picador, 1988, originally published as *Le deuxième sexe*, 1949). She says of this group of writers that 'well aware of their own oppression', they use their gifts as creative writers to fulfil themselves as women (*In Search of Our Mothers' Gardens*, p. 251).

As a student, Walker read all the Russian novels she could. She learned from Leo Tolstoy (1828–1910) 'to drive through' political and social issues to reach the individual spirit, an effort needed to make characters live (*In Search of Our Mothers' Gardens*, p. 257). She admired the other great Russians of the nineteenth century, but was disappointed to find no Russian women novelists. Among poets, she enjoyed the Americans Emily Dickinson (1830–86) and e.e. cummings (1894–1962), and the British poet Robert Graves (1895–1985), champion of the White (Moon) Goddess, who represents the creative female principle, long suppressed by male rationalising (*In Search of Our Mothers' Gardens*, p. 257). *The Temple of My Familiar* is dedicated 'To Robert, in whom the Goddess shines'. She also speaks of her enjoyment of the 'sensual' Latin poems of Catullus (*c.*84–*c.*54BC) and Ovid (43BC–AD17), and of Japanese haiku poets, who taught her the possibilities of short forms.

CONTEXT
Womanists love the moon because of the Moon Goddess, championed by Robert Graves.

Among African writers, she praises the Nigerian, Elechi Amadi (b.1934), whose novel *The Concubine* (1966) may have influenced her story 'Roselily', a prototype of *The Color Purple*, and the distinguished South African novelist Bessie Head (1937–86), whose conviction that God is known in Africa in ways undreamt of by missionaries may have influenced the presentation of religious themes in Walker's fiction.

The Color Purple belongs to the genre of **epistolary** novels. The greatest writer in this tradition was one of the earliest, Samuel Richardson (1689–1761). The novel in letters appealed to women novelists, including Mrs Aphra Behn (1640–89) and Fanny Burney (1752–1840). Jane Austen (1775–1817) also experimented with novels in the form of letters. There have been novels of this kind in the modern period, but the invention of the telephone seems to have impaired the already somewhat restricted nature of the genre. Alice Walker may have had in mind her predecessors among female novelists, but she may also have intended to remind us of Richardson's vast and enthralling novels *Pamela* (1740–1) and *Clarissa* (1747–8), which deal with the plight of women insulted and abused by villainous men. Like Jean Toomer, Richardson was a man with a strong and delicate sensibility.

SPIELBERG'S FILM, *THE COLOR PURPLE*

Alice Walker has mixed feelings about Steven Spielberg's film, *The Color Purple* (1985), on which she worked as a consultant. At one time she wanted it to have a different title, to distance it from her novel. She regrets the omission from the film of the sexual relations (except for an occasional kiss) between Celie and Shug. She writes warmly, however, in her memoir *The Same River Twice* (which has much to say about the film), of the performances of Whoopi Goldberg as Celie, Margaret Avery as Shug and Oprah Winfrey as Sofia. She also praises the music and songs, which contribute powerfully to the film. She commends especially the song 'Sister', written by Quincy Jones, Rod Templeton and Lionel Richie, calling it 'an immeasurable gift to the bonding of women' – and only regretting (a little) that it was composed by brothers.

 CHECK THE BOOK

There is a chapter on this film in James Clarke, *The Pocket Essential Steven Spielberg* (2001).

CONTEXT

Alice Walker commented, 'I sat up most of the night reading and pondering the enormous significance of Harriet Wilson's novel *Our Nig'*.

Some scenes in the film are both dramatically effective and closely modelled on the book. These include Sofia's hitting the mayor and Miss Millie's attempt to take Sofia home for Christmas. Although much detail inevitably has to be omitted, the film can recreate in a single image an effect the novelist worked to convey over many pages. The mailbox makes good symbolic appearances in the film (see **Symbolism**). Spielberg makes good use of hands clapping and touching, and of sunlight ('Watch for Me in the Sunset' was Walker's idea for an alternative title).

Other scenes are very convincing but alter the novel's action and timing of events. Celie's encounter with Corrine in the store, for example, shows what a shop in the Georgia of that time would have looked like, and lets us hear the rude voice of the white 'clerk', but the child Olivia, six years old in the novel, is a baby. A dramatic sequence in the film alternates shots of Celie standing behind Albert with his razor in her hand with shots of Adam and Tashi undergoing the ceremony of ritual scarring in Africa. The circumstances are different in the book. Walker's Celie is not required to shave Albert and Shug is present with them in the room, while in the film she races to the house to stop Celie; Tashi and Adam are scarred as children in the film, as adults in the novel. Tashi and Adam undergo the ceremony on separate occasions in the novel, and years after the time when Celie wants to kill Albert.

Serious novelists have always tended to find that film treatments of their work involve other (that is, not artistic) alterations with a view to attracting the biggest possible audience. There are changes of this sort throughout Spielberg's film. These remind us of how disturbing the novel is to many sorts of settled opinion and taste. Much of the sexual violence of the novel is omitted on the screen. The rape of Celie reported in the first letter is not shown. The film opens with pictures of Celie and Nettie romping happily in purple-tinted fields. Celie's hard labour in squalid conditions during her early years with Albert is also omitted or much subdued. Walker's Celie is in rags when Albert's sisters visit her; Spielberg's Celie is always decently dressed. Domestic life in the film is too cosy. Conventional Hollywood scenes, such as Albert's trying to cook Shug's breakfast, occupy more time than episodes of greater interest, such as the whole marital struggle of Harpo and Sofia. The novel's feminist themes and the strictures on colonialism are considerably muted. The film's Africa is one of elephants, giraffes and vaguely-pictured tribesmen, in a different physical setting (Kenya) from the one Walker describes (West Africa).

The result was a commercially successful film, which left the novelist and many of her admirers partly disappointed.

CONTEXT

Spielberg's film won eleven Oscar nominations, but no awards.

CONTEXT

Toni Morrison's *Beloved* won the Pulitzer Prize.

World events	Alice Walker	Literary events
		1740-1 Samuel Richardson, *Pamela*
1822 Liberia is founded as a colony for freed slaves		
1834 Slavery is abolished in the British Empire		
1841 David Livingstone begins missionary work in Africa		
		1851-2 Harriet Beecher Stowe, *Uncle Tom's Cabin*
1857 Dakar founded		
1858 John Hanning Speke becomes first European to see Lake Victoria		
1861 Civil war breaks out in North America		
1865 End of the American Civil War; slavery is abolished in the USA		
1866 Ex-slaves granted citizenship and equal rights; Ku Klux Klan founded		
1871 Henry Morton Stanley finds David Livingstone near Lake Tanganyika		
		1881-1910 Joel Chandler Harris, *Uncle Remus* series
1884-1966 Sophie Tucker, black American singer, actress and entertainer		**1884** Mark Twain, *Huckleberry Finn*
1890-1912 Various Southern States pass 'Jim Crow' laws to segregate whites and blacks; all Southern States passed laws imposing requirements for voting that were used to prevent blacks from voting		
1894-1937 Bessie Smith, black American singer		
1899-1974 Duke Ellington, black American bandleader		
		1903 W. E. B. Du Bois, *The Souls of Black Folk*

World events	Alice Walker	Literary events
1905 Niagra movement founded in the USA		
1908 Belgium takes possession of Belgian Congo		
1909 National Association for the Advancement of Colored People founded in the USA		
1914-18 World War I – blacks were enlisted to fight for the USA, though they were still segregated		
		1923 Jean Toomer, *Cane*
1929 Wall Street Crash		
1930 The black nationalist separatist organisation, The Nation of Islam, is founded		
		1937 Zora Neale Hurston, *Their Eyes Were Watching God*
1938 Supreme Court ruled that the state of Missouri was obliged to provide access to a public law school for blacks, just as it provided for whites		
	1944 Born in Eatonton, Georgia	
		1949 Simone de Beauvoir, *The Second Sex*
		1951 J. D. Salinger, *The Catcher in the Rye*
1954 Supreme Court stated that racially segregated education was unconstitutional		
1956 In Montgomery, Alabama, Rosa Parks refuses to give up her bus seat to a white man leading to mass boycotts and the start of the Civil Rights Movement		
1957 Martin Luther King becomes president of the newly founded Southern Christian Leadership Conference		

World events	Alice Walker	Literary events
		1959 Lorraine Vivian Hansberry, *A Raisin in the Sun*
	1961 Begins studies at Spelman College, Atlanta, Georgia	
		1962 Doris Lessing, *The Golden Notebook*
	1963 Transfers to Sarah Lawrence College, New York	
1964 Congress passes the Civil Rights Act banning segregation		
1965 Race riots occur throughout the USA in protest against economic and social conditions; USA sends troops to Vietnam	**1965** Graduates; wins writing scholarship for following year	
		1966 Margaret Walker, *Jubilee*; Elechi Amadi, *The Concubine*
	1967 Marries Melvyn R. Levanthal, a Civil Rights lawyer; Alice's essay 'The Civil Rights Movement: What Good Was It?' wins a prize offered by American Scholar; publishes her first short story 'To Hell With Dying'	
1968 Martin Luther King is assassinated; the militant Black Panther organisation is founded to promote the armed self protection of black communities	**1968** Publishes her first collection of poems, *Once: Poems*	
	1969 Rebecca, her daughter, is born	
	1970 Publishes her first novel, *The Third Life of Grange Copeland*	**1970** Toni Morrison, *The Bluest Eye*
1972 Equal Opportunity Act leads to extension of affirmative action to colleges and universities		

World events	Alice Walker	Literary events
	1973 *Love and Trouble Stories of Black Women*	**1973** Toni Morrison, *Sula*
1974 Nixon resigns	**1974** *Langston Hughes: American Poet*	
1975 USA withdraws from Vietnam		
1976 Riots in Soweto, South Africa	**1976** Alice and Melvyn are divorced; *Meridian*	
1977 Public Works Employment Act ensures 10% of contractors on public works must be from minorities		**1977** Ama Ata Aidoo, *Our Sister Killjoy*
	1981 *You Can't Keep a Good Woman Down*	**1981** Toni Morrison, *Tar Baby*
	1982 *The Color Purple* is published	**1982** Gloria Naylor, *The Women of Brewster Place*
	1983 *In Search of Our Mothers' Gardens: Womanist Prose*; becomes first black woman to win the Pulitzer Prize for literature	
	1985 Steven Spielberg's film of *The Color Purple* opens; co-founds Wild Trees Press publishing company	
		1987 Toni Morrison, *Beloved*
	1989 *The Temple of My Familiar*	**1989** Buchi Emecheta, *Gwendolen*
1990 Nelson Mandela released from twenty-seven years imprisonment		
	1992 *Possessing the Secret of Joy*	**1992** Toni Morrison, *Jazz* and *Playing in the Dark: Whiteness and the Literary Imagination*
	1993 *Warrior Marks* (book and film) with Pratibha Parmer	
1994 Nelson Mandela becomes President of South Africa		

FURTHER READING

ALICE WALKER'S OTHER BOOKS

The Temple of My Familiar, Harcourt Brace Jovanovich, New York, 1989, and The Women's Press, London.
Sequel to *The Color Purple*

Possessing the Secret of Joy, Harcourt Brace Jovanovich, New York, 1992, and The Women's Press, London.

In Search of Our Mothers' Gardens: Womanist Prose (1983).
Essays

The Same River Twice: Honoring the Difficult: A Meditation on Life, Spirit, Art, and the Making of the Film The Color Purple Ten Years Later (1996).
Full of relevant and interesting ideas

I Love Myself When I am Laughing: A Zora Neale Hurston Reader (Feminist Press, New York, 1979).
For an introduction to Zora Neale Hurston, the black American writer to whom Alice Walker is most indebted

BACKGROUND READING

Chinua Achebe, *Things Fall Apart*, Heinemann, London, 1958
A start on African fiction in English

bell hooks, 'Writing the Subject: Reading *The Color Purple*', from Henry Louis Gates Jnr (ed.), *Reading Black, Reading Feminist: A Critical Anthology,* Meridian, New York, 1990

Renée C. Hoogland, 'Heterosexual Screening: Lesbian Studies', from R. Buikema. and A. Smelik (eds), *Women's Studies and Culture: A Feminist Introduction*, Zed Books, London and New Jersey, 1995
This collection, which first appeared in Dutch in 1993, includes Liesbeth Brouwer's essay, 'The Colour of the Sign: Feminist semiotics', quoted in **Critical history**, and other discussions of *The Color Purple* from several feminist viewpoints, including literary theory, linguistics, film studies, art history and musicology

Toni Morrison, *The Bluest Eye (1970), Sula* (1973) and *Tar Baby* (1981) and *Beloved* (1987) Chatto and Windus, London.

Andrea Stuart, '*The Color Purple*: In Defence of Happy Endings' in L. Gamman and M. Marshment (eds), *The Female Gaze: Women as Viewers of Popular Culture*, The Women's Press, London, 1988.
A critical essay in appreciation of the novel and a discussion of the film

SLAVE NARRATIVES

Angela Davis, *Women, Race and Class*, The Women's Press, London, 1982.
> Information about women's involvement in the struggle to end slavery in the nineteenth century, slave narratives and the famous 'Ain't I a Woman?' speech by Sojourner Truth

Harriet A. Jacobs, *Incidents in the Life of a Slave Girl: Written by Herself*, (re-edited and introduced) Jean Fagan Yellin, Oxford University Press, Oxford, 1988.
> First published under a pseudonym in 1861. Such books, once ephemeral-seeming productions on the margins of literature, have been rescued and restored to our attention. They are full of interest for readers of Alice Walker

Sandi Russell, *Render Me My Song: African American Women Writers from Slavery to the Present*, St Martin's Press, New York, 1992.
> Students exploring the history of black American literature should consult this book which has a useful bibliography. Russell provides a clear, helpful introduction, beginning with the poet and ex-slave Phillis Wheatley (1753-84); Zora Neale Hurston has a chapter to herself; later parts of the book are devoted to Toni Morrison, Alice Walker and their contemporaries

Harriet E. Wilson, Henry Louis Gates, Jr, (ed), *Our Nig; or, Sketches from the Life of A Free Black,* first published anonymously in 1859, Vintage Books, New York, 1983).
> The African-American scholar has brought to light two books by women. Gates's introduction to his new edition explains 'the disappearance and reappearance' of this novel by a former slave, and brings out the significance of its ironic title

See also Hannah Crafts, *The Bondwoman's Narrative*
> Another novel by a fugitive slave, which has recently been published for the first time. Gates's introduction tells how he discovered the manuscript

LITERARY TERMS

alliteration a pattern in which one consonant is repeated, as in 'Five miles meandering with a mazy motion', or two or more alternate, as in 'And rents were lower in Rawlinson Road'

black today a cultural and political term, which makes no reference to skin colour, although it sometimes does so refer in the speech of characters in the novel

closure the sense of an ending, happy, tragic or thoughtful, which marks the close of a story or play; deliberately unfinished or unresolved stories are sometimes said to be 'open-ended'

ellipsis omission of words normally required by grammar for literary effect, as in 'He for God only, she for God in him', where the verbs are missing

epistolary in the form of letters

gender in feminist writings, now refers to sexual identity seen as the product of social and cultural influences, rather than to biological difference

historic present (tense) use of present tense to relate past events to create a sense of immediacy

imagery an image is (i) a picture created by words, as in 'the image of Olivia passing on her lessons to Tashi' (ii) a metaphor or a simile, as in 'she smile, like a razor opening'

melodrama a sensational story with violent and improbable events

morpheme the smallest meaningful unit of speech, either a word, such as 'fair' or a part of a word such as 'un' in 'unfair' or 'ly' in 'fairly'

oral culture one in which myths and legends, jokes and proverbs, folk tales and ballads and all components of the culture are remembered and repeated rather than written down

pantheist believes that God is in everything or that God is the universe. In America, Ralph Waldo Emerson (1803–82) spread belief in an ultimate spiritual revelation of the union of mind and nature, in opposition to the Christian belief that God created nature

patriarchy originally, rule by the fathers (of the tribe). In feminist criticism, refers to ways in which culture is organised according to masculine values

phonaesthemic relating sound and meaning through association. The monosyllabic phonaestheme 'Shug' may be grouped with 'shove', 'shun', 'shush', 'shut', 'shuffle', 'shucks', or with a group including 'shrug' or another including 'hug', to try to identify an English-speaker's feeling for the name

point of view in first-person narratives the narrator, usually one of the characters, tells the story from his or her point of view, using 'I'. In a novel in letters, the point of view changes with the letter-writer

realism a tendency, strong in nineteenth-century novels, sceptically regarded by many modern writers, to aim to convey the actual experience of ordinary life. It can be thought of as the opposite of fantasy or escapism. It is, however, a flexible and slippery term

rhetoric(al) devices in the art of public speaking, often suspect in Western culture today, but respected in Africa and by African-American preachers and politicians. 'Ain't I a woman?', reiterated in Sojourner Truth's famous speech, was a rhetorical question, since everyone could see that she was

slave narrative the autobiography of a former slave. See *Six Women's Slave Narratives* (Oxford University Press, New York and Oxford, 1988)

stream of consciousness a technique in modern narrative which abandons composition in properly formed sentences in order to try to catch the flow of a character's thoughts and feelings

AUTHOR OF THESE NOTES

Neil McEwan read English at Pembroke College, Oxford, and taught English literature at universities in many parts of the world, including England, Canada, Cameroon and Japan. He is now a freelance writer, based in England. He has published several critical studies, including *The Survival of the Novel* (1981), *Africa and the Novel* (1983), *Perspective in British Historical Fiction Today* (1987), and *Graham Greene* (1988) and *Anthony Powell* (1991) in the 'Macmillan Modern Novelists' series. He edited Volume 5, *The Twentieth Century*, in *The Macmillan Anthologies of English Literature* (1989). He is the author of *Style in English Prose* (1986) and *Preparing for Examinations in English Literature* (1982) in York Handbooks.

General editors

Martin Gray, former Head of the Department of English Studies at the University of Stirling, and of Literary Studies at the University of Luton

Professor A. N. Jeffares, Emeritus Professor of English, University of Stirling

Maya Angelou
I Know Why the Caged Bird Sings

Jane Austen
Pride and Prejudice

Alan Ayckbourn
Absent Friends

Elizabeth Barrett Browning
Selected Poems

Robert Bolt
A Man for All Seasons

Harold Brighouse
Hobson's Choice

Charlotte Brontë
Jane Eyre

Emily Brontë
Wuthering Heights

Shelagh Delaney
A Taste of Honey

Charles Dickens
David Copperfield
Great Expectations
Hard Times
Oliver Twist

Roddy Doyle
Paddy Clarke Ha Ha Ha

George Eliot
Silas Marner
The Mill on the Floss

Anne Frank
The Diary of a Young Girl

William Golding
Lord of the Flies

Oliver Goldsmith
She Stoops to Conquer

Willis Hall
The Long and the Short and the Tall

Thomas Hardy
Far from the Madding Crowd
The Mayor of Casterbridge
Tess of the d'Urbervilles
The Withered Arm and other Wessex Tales

L.P. Hartley
The Go-Between

Seamus Heaney
Selected Poems

Susan Hill
I'm the King of the Castle

Barry Hines
A Kestrel for a Knave

Louise Lawrence
Children of the Dust

Harper Lee
To Kill a Mockingbird

Laurie Lee
Cider with Rosie

Arthur Miller
The Crucible
A View from the Bridge

Robert O'Brien
Z for Zachariah

Frank O'Connor
My Oedipus Complex and Other Stories

George Orwell
Animal Farm

J.B. Priestley
An Inspector Calls
When We Are Married

Willy Russell
Educating Rita
Our Day Out

J.D. Salinger
The Catcher in the Rye

William Shakespeare
Henry IV Part I
Henry V
Julius Caesar
Macbeth
The Merchant of Venice
A Midsummer Night's Dream
Much Ado About Nothing

Romeo and Juliet
The Tempest
Twelfth Night

George Bernard Shaw
Pygmalion

Mary Shelley
Frankenstein

R.C. Sherriff
Journey's End

Rukshana Smith
Salt on the snow

John Steinbeck
Of Mice and Men

Robert Louis Stevenson
Dr Jekyll and Mr Hyde

Jonathan Swift
Gulliver's Travels

Robert Swindells
Daz 4 Zoe

Mildred D. Taylor
Roll of Thunder, Hear My Cry

Mark Twain
Huckleberry Finn

James Watson
Talking in Whispers

Edith Wharton
Ethan Frome

William Wordsworth
Selected Poems

A Choice of Poets

Mystery Stories of the Nineteenth Century including The Signalman

Nineteenth Century Short Stories

Poetry of the First World War

Six Women Poets

For the AQA Anthology:

Duffy and Armitage & Pre-1914 Poetry

Heaney and Clarke & Pre-1914 Poetry

Poems from Different Cultures

Margaret Atwood
Cat's Eye
The Handmaid's Tale

Jane Austen
Emma
Mansfield Park
Persuasion
Pride and Prejudice
Sense and Sensibility

Alan Bennett
Talking Heads

William Blake
Songs of Innocence and of Experience

Charlotte Brontë
Jane Eyre
Villette

Emily Brontë
Wuthering Heights

Angela Carter
Nights at the Circus

Geoffrey Chaucer
The Franklin's Prologue and Tale
The Merchant's Prologue and Tale
The Miller's Prologue and Tale
The Prologue to the Canterbury Tales
The Wife of Bath's Prologue and Tale

Samuel Coleridge
Selected Poems

Joseph Conrad
Heart of Darkness

Daniel Defoe
Moll Flanders

Charles Dickens
Bleak House
Great Expectations
Hard Times

Emily Dickinson
Selected Poems

John Donne
Selected Poems

Carol Ann Duffy
Selected Poems

George Eliot
Middlemarch
The Mill on the Floss

T.S. Eliot
Selected Poems
The Waste Land

F. Scott Fitzgerald
The Great Gatsby

E.M. Forster
A Passage to India

Brian Friel
Translations

Thomas Hardy
Jude the Obscure
The Mayor of Casterbridge
The Return of the Native
Selected Poems
Tess of the d'Urbervilles

Seamus Heaney
Selected Poems from 'Opened Ground'

Nathaniel Hawthorne
The Scarlet Letter

Homer
The Iliad
The Odyssey

Aldous Huxley
Brave New World

Kazuo Ishiguro
The Remains of the Day

Ben Jonson
The Alchemist

James Joyce
Dubliners

John Keats
Selected Poems

Philip Larkin
The Whitsun Weddings and Selected Poems

Christopher Marlowe
Doctor Faustus
Edward II

Arthur Miller
Death of a Salesman

John Milton
Paradise Lost Books I & II

Toni Morrison
Beloved

George Orwell
Nineteen Eighty-Four

Sylvia Plath
Selected Poems

Alexander Pope
Rape of the Lock & Selected Poems

William Shakespeare
Antony and Cleopatra
As You Like It
Hamlet
Henry IV Part I
King Lear
Macbeth
Measure for Measure
The Merchant of Venice
A Midsummer Night's Dream
Much Ado About Nothing
Othello
Richard II
Richard III
Romeo and Juliet
The Taming of the Shrew
The Tempest
Twelfth Night
The Winter's Tale

George Bernard Shaw
Saint Joan

Mary Shelley
Frankenstein

Jonathan Swift
Gulliver's Travels and A Modest Proposal

Alfred Tennyson
Selected Poems

Virgil
The Aeneid

Alice Walker
The Color Purple

Oscar Wilde
The Importance of Being Earnest

Tennessee Williams
A Streetcar Named Desire
The Glass Menagerie

Jeanette Winterson
Oranges Are Not the Only Fruit

John Webster
The Duchess of Malfi

Virginia Woolf
To the Lighthouse

William Wordsworth
The Prelude and Selected Poems

W.B. Yeats
Selected Poems

Metaphysical Poets

THE ULTIMATE WEB SITE FOR THE ULTIMATE LITERATURE GUIDES

At York Notes we believe in helping you achieve exam success. Log on to **www.yorknotes.com** and see how we have made revision even easier, with over 300 titles available to download twenty-four hours a day. The downloads have lots of additional features such as pop-up boxes providing instant glossary definitions, user-friendly links to every part of the guide, and scanned illustrations offering visual appeal. All you need to do is log on to **www.yorknotes.com** and download the books you need to help you achieve exam success.

KEY FEATURES:

Details on how York Notes can help you

Menu Bar to help you find your way around the site

Details on how to download York Notes

Quick Search facility to help you find the titles you need

Link to news about new titles

List of top-selling downloads